AF183060

Family Planning, Women's Empowerment, and Population and Societal Impacts

PROCEEDINGS OF A WORKSHOP

Caroline Sferrazza, *Rapporteur*

Committee on Population

Division of Behavioral and Social Sciences and Education

The National Academies of
SCIENCES · ENGINEERING · MEDICINE

THE NATIONAL ACADEMIES PRESS
Washington, DC
www.nap.edu

THE NATIONAL ACADEMIES PRESS 500 Fifth Street, NW Washington, DC 20001

This activity was supported by a contract between the National Academy of Sciences and the Bill & Melinda Gates Foundation, award # OPP1216711. Additional support was provided by the National Academy of Sciences W.K. Kellogg Foundation Fund. Any opinions, findings, conclusions, or recommendations expressed in this publication do not necessarily reflect the views of any organization or agency that provided support for the project.

International Standard Book Number-13: 978-0-309-14900-6
International Standard Book Number-10: 0-309-14900-2
Digital Object Identifier: https://doi.org/10.17226/26023

Additional copies of this publication are available from the National Academies Press, 500 Fifth Street, NW, Keck 360, Washington, DC 20001; (800) 624-6242 or (202) 334-3313; http://www.nap.edu.

Copyright 2021 by the National Academy of Sciences. All rights reserved.

Printed in the United States of America

Suggested citation: National Academies of Sciences, Engineering, and Medicine. (2021). *Family Planning, Women's Empowerment, and Population and Societal Impacts: Proceedings of a Workshop*. Washington, DC: The National Academies Press. https://doi.org/10.17226/26023.

The National Academies of
SCIENCES • ENGINEERING • MEDICINE

The **National Academy of Sciences** was established in 1863 by an Act of Congress, signed by President Lincoln, as a private, nongovernmental institution to advise the nation on issues related to science and technology. Members are elected by their peers for outstanding contributions to research. Dr. Marcia McNutt is president.

The **National Academy of Engineering** was established in 1964 under the charter of the National Academy of Sciences to bring the practices of engineering to advising the nation. Members are elected by their peers for extraordinary contributions to engineering. Dr. John L. Anderson is president.

The **National Academy of Medicine** (formerly the Institute of Medicine) was established in 1970 under the charter of the National Academy of Sciences to advise the nation on medical and health issues. Members are elected by their peers for distinguished contributions to medicine and health. Dr. Victor J. Dzau is president.

The three Academies work together as the **National Academies of Sciences, Engineering, and Medicine** to provide independent, objective analysis and advice to the nation and conduct other activities to solve complex problems and inform public policy decisions. The National Academies also encourage education and research, recognize outstanding contributions to knowledge, and increase public understanding in matters of science, engineering, and medicine.

Learn more about the National Academies of Sciences, Engineering, and Medicine at **www.nationalacademies.org**.

The National Academies of
SCIENCES • ENGINEERING • MEDICINE

Consensus Study Reports published by the National Academies of Sciences, Engineering, and Medicine document the evidence-based consensus on the study's statement of task by an authoring committee of experts. Reports typically include findings, conclusions, and recommendations based on information gathered by the committee and the committee's deliberations. Each report has been subjected to a rigorous and independent peer-review process and it represents the position of the National Academies on the statement of task.

Proceedings published by the National Academies of Sciences, Engineering, and Medicine chronicle the presentations and discussions at a workshop, symposium, or other event convened by the National Academies. The statements and opinions contained in proceedings are those of the participants and are not endorsed by other participants, the planning committee, or the National Academies.

For information about other products and activities of the National Academies, please visit www.nationalacademies.org/about/whatwedo.

STEERING COMMITTEE CALL FOR THE WORKSHOP ON FAMILY PLANNING, WOMEN'S EMPOWERMENT, AND POPULATION AND SOCIETAL IMPACTS

ANN K. BLANC (*Chair*), Population Council
NANCY BIRDSALL, Center for Global Development
MAYRA BUVINIC, United Nations Foundation
ALEX EZEH, Drexel University
JOCELYN FINLAY, Harvard University
SUNITA KISHOR, ICF
AMY ONG TSUI, Johns Hopkins University (emerita)

KRISZTINA MARTON, *Study Director*
ELLIS GRIMES, *Senior Program Assistant*
MALAY MAJMUNDAR, *Director, Committee on Population*

COMMITTEE ON POPULATION

KATHLEEN MULLAN HARRIS (*Chair*), University of North Carolina at Chapel Hill
LISA F. BERKMAN, Harvard T.H. Chan School of Public Health
NANCY BIRDSALL, Center for Global Development
ANN K. BLANC, The Population Council
VICKI A. FREEDMAN, University of Michigan
DANA A. GLEI, Georgetown University
ROBERT A. HUMMER, University of North Carolina at Chapel Hill
HILLARD S. KAPLAN, Chapman University
HEDWIG LEE, Washington University
JENNIFER J. MANLY, Columbia University Medical Center
EMILIO A. PARRADO, University of Pennsylvania
ISABEL V. SAWHILL, The Brookings Institution
JOHN R. WILMOTH, United Nations
REBECCA WONG, University of Texas Medical Branch at Galveston

MALAY MAJMUNDAR, *Director*

Acknowledgments

This Proceedings of a Workshop was reviewed in draft form by individuals chosen for their diverse perspectives and technical expertise. The purpose of this independent review is to provide candid and critical comments that will assist the National Academies of Sciences, Engineering, and Medicine in making each published proceedings as sound as possible and to ensure that it meets the institutional standards for quality, objectivity, evidence, and responsiveness to the charge. The review comments and draft manuscript remain confidential to protect the integrity of the process.

We thank the following individuals for their review of this proceedings: Jere Behrman, University of Pennsylvania and Amy Tsui, Johns Hopkins University (emerita). Although the reviewers provided many constructive comments and suggestions, they were not asked to endorse the content of the proceedings nor did they see the final draft before its release.

The review of this proceedings was overseen by Anne R. Pebley, University of California, Los Angeles. She was responsible for making certain that an independent examination of this proceedings was carried out in accordance with standards of the National Academies and that all review comments were carefully considered.

This meeting summary was prepared by Caroline Sferrazza, Rose Li and Associates, Inc. Dana Carluccio and Nancy Tuvesson from Rose Li and Associates reviewed earlier versions. Responsibility for the final content rests entirely with the rapporteur and the National Academies.

Contents

1

Introduction

BACKGROUND

This Proceedings of a Workshop summarizes the presentations and discussions held at the Workshop on Family Planning, Women's Empowerment, and Population and Societal Impacts, which took place virtually in September 2020 and was made available in real time by public webcast. The workshop was convened with support from the Bill & Melinda Gates Foundation, and it was organized by a seven-member planning committee appointed by the National Academies of Sciences, Engineering, and Medicine.

Over the past several decades, fertility rates have fallen substantially in low- and middle-income countries, and efforts to limit fertility, primarily through the implementation of family planning programs, have become increasingly widespread. Although there is a substantial scholarly literature on the determinants of contraceptive use and other measures to limit fertility and on the resulting differentials in fertility, relatively little is known about the role played by women's empowerment as both a determinant and a consequence of fertility decline. In addition, there continues to be little consensus about the link between fertility decline and broader societal impacts, including economic development.

The goal of this workshop was to bring together experts and stakeholders to discuss conceptual, methodological, and policy issues regarding the relationships among family planning, women's empowerment, fertility decline, and population and societal impacts. The discussion was intended to inform research and policy focused on the issues of women's roles and empowerment and on longstanding questions surrounding the determinants and consequences of fertility reduction behavior.

WORKSHOP FOCUS

Box 1-1 contains the workshop's statement of task. In his introductory remarks, Win Brown (Bill & Melinda Gates Foundation) framed the workshop as a revisitation of questions and themes explored in the 1986 National Research Council report on population growth and economic development.[1] The modern context for this revisitation includes recent population projections by the Institute for Health Metrics and Evaluation, which forecasts a decline in the global total fertility rate by 2100. Brown explained that the scholars in attendance at this workshop could provide valuable insights into the factors that have influenced these projections (e.g., women's empowerment, modern contraceptive prevalence) and how those factors affect the foundational questions posed in the landmark 1986 report. Brown quoted the late U.S. Supreme Court Justice, Ruth Bader Ginsburg, who passed away less than 1 week before the workshop took place: "The decision whether or not to bear a child is central to a woman's life—to her well-being and dignity. It is a decision she must make for herself."[2] Brown described the influence that Ginsburg's work had on the themes of this workshop, and sought to contextualize the workshop's proceedings by reminding participants of both the importance and fragility of the research subjects under discussion.

ORGANIZATION OF THE REPORT

This summary describes the workshop presentations and discussions that took place at the end of each session. The chapters are organized around the sessions of the workshop, which included the role of fertility decline and women's empowerment in economic development and in other population and societal changes; measuring women's empowerment; ways of addressing current data limitations; family planning, fertility, and women's empowerment in low- and middle-income countries; and mechanisms of attitude change. The workshop also included a discussion with representatives of organizations and agencies that fund work in this area,

---

[1] Working Group on Population Growth and Economic Development, Committee on Population, Commission on Behavioral and Social Sciences and Education, National Research Council, *Population Growth and Economic Development: Policy Questions* (Washington, DC: National Academy Press, 1986).

[2] The quotation is from Ginsburg's testimony to the United States Senate during her confirmation hearing for a seat on the Supreme Court, August 3, 1993.

and a discussion of key themes and next steps by members of the workshop planning committee. The full meeting agenda is shown in the Appendix.

These proceedings have been prepared by the workshop rapporteur as a factual summary of what occurred at the workshop. The planning committee's role was limited to planning and convening the workshop. The views contained in the proceedings are those of individual workshop participants and do not necessarily represent the views of all workshop participants, the planning committee, or the National Academies of Sciences, Engineering, and Medicine.

BOX 1-1
Workshop Statement of Task

An ad hoc planning committee will plan and execute a 2-day workshop that will bring together experts and stakeholders to discuss conceptual, methodological, and policy issues regarding the relationship between family planning, women's empowerment, and population and societal impacts. Questions that could be addressed during the workshop include

- What are the ways in which women's empowerment is measured and operationalized?
- What are the key data sources for studying the relationship between contraceptive use, fertility, and women's empowerment? What are the key data limitations, and how might they be addressed?
- What are the mechanisms by which changes in attitudes toward and opportunities for girls and women affect changes in attitudes toward and use of contraceptives—and vice versa?
- To what extent does the nexus between family planning, fertility, and women's empowerment vary within and across low- and middle-income countries?
- What is the link between women's empowerment, fertility decline, and other population and societal impacts?

The planning committee will define the specific topics to be addressed, develop the agenda, and invite speakers and other participants. After the workshop, proceedings of the workshop will be prepared by a designated rapporteur in accordance with institutional guidelines.

2

The Role of Fertility Decline and Women's Empowerment in Economic Development and in Other Population and Societal Changes

Points Highlighted by the Presenters

- The nexus between fertility and women's labor force participation varies significantly within and across low- and middle-income countries. Access to family planning influences these relationships, but precisely how it does so could be better understood. (Jocelyn Finlay, Harvard University)
- It is important to distinguish between different kinds of agency (e.g., capabilities, empowerment, citizenship), as they have differing implications for structural inequalities. (Naila Kabeer, London School of Economics)
- Although traditional policies to improve women's labor market outcomes (e.g., training, microcredit, education) are important, more labor market policies could be developed that specifically operate on gender norms. (Seema Jayachandran, Northwestern University)

Amy Tsui (Johns Hopkins University, emerita) served as moderator for this session and explained that the presenters were asked to consider the following questions in their presentations:

- What is the link between fertility change and economic development, especially at the macro level?
- What is the role of women's empowerment as an intervening variable?

- What do we know about the relationship between changes in the role and status of women in developing countries and economic growth?
- Has access to family planning mattered?

REPRODUCTIVE HEALTH AND WOMEN'S ECONOMIC ACTIVITY: A NARRATIVE REVIEW

Jocelyn Finlay (Harvard University) addressed two key questions: To what extent does the nexus between fertility and women's labor force participation (LFP) vary within and across low- and middle-income countries, and does access to family planning matter for women's LFP? Finlay explained that her discussion of these questions was based upon a manuscript currently under review,[1] would not include discussion of gender norms, and would not assume that women's LFP is inherently empowering.

The connection between fertility and women's LFP varies greatly across income groups and continents, Finlay noted. Women's LFP itself varies both in rate and in type across a country's income levels.[2] Of all working women in low- and middle-income countries, approximately 90 percent and 50 percent, respectively, work in the informal sector, that is, in jobs that are unregulated by the government. The fertility rate also differs between low- and middle-income countries, with an average of 4.5 children per woman and 2.5 children per woman, respectively. The interaction of income and fertility has been illustrated in the "quality-quantity trade-off" model, in which families that earn higher incomes choose to have smaller numbers of "higher quality" children (e.g., children who are healthier and more educated).[3] Finlay thus links fertility and women's LFP by extending the quality-quantity trade-off to explain that with fewer children, women have more time available to participate in the workforce. This theory would predict an inverse relationship between the number of children and women's LFP, yet Finlay finds that the relationship is not so straightforward in reality.

In sub-Saharan African low-income countries, the number of children and LFP can be directly related for some women: their labor participation

---

[1] J.E. Finlay, Women's reproductive health and economic activity: A narrative review (in press).

[2] C. Goldin, The U-shaped female labor force function in economic development and economic history (pp. 61–90 in *Investment in Women's Human Capital and Economic Development*, edited by T.P. Schultz, Chicago: University of Chicago Press, 1995).

[3] G.S. Becker and H.G. Lewis, On the interaction between the quantity and quality of children, *Journal of Political Economy 81*(2), S279–S288.

increases upon the birth of a child.[4] Finlay noted that this pattern may be explained by a lack of income sharing in the household, that is, that incomes from husbands and wives are not pooled. In low-income countries where women are responsible for all the costs associated with a child (e.g., food, clothing, health, education), they must work to cover those expenses. Because 90 percent of these working mothers are employed in the informal sector, they lack the social safety nets (e.g., maternity leave, childcare subsidies, tax breaks) that would allow a healthy balance between child-rearing and work. Therefore, women in low-income countries achieve increased LFP by relying on their older children to care for younger siblings and/or practicing long birth spacing.[5]

In South Asian low-income countries, however, a quite different relationship exists between LFP and fertility. In these countries, a nonlinear relationship between women's LFP and fertility has been observed.[6] Finlay highlighted gender norms that restrict women's access to the labor market (regardless of whether or not they have children) as a central driver of this observed difference.[7]

The relationship between fertility and women's LFP in Latin American middle-income countries is heterogeneous. Although studies have demonstrated a causal effect of fertility on women's LFP, Finlay noted that the impact of high rates of income inequality is not considered in these investigations. She cited a study from Mayra Buvinic (United Nations Foundation)—which found that teen motherhood had no effect on LFP in teen mothers from rich households but *increased* LFP in teen mothers from poor households—as an example of the heterogenous relationship between fertility and LFP in middle-income countries.[8] In this case, the finding may be explained by the increased likelihood that a teen mother would also act as the head of household in poorer families. Finlay highlighted single motherhood, income inequality, and inequality in labor market opportunity as worthy avenues for future exploration.

[4] R. Heath and S. Jayachandran, *The Causes and Consequences of Increased Female Education and Labor Force Participation in Developing Countries*, NBER Working Paper No. 22766 (Cambridge, MA: National Bureau of Economic Research, 2017).

[5] J.E. Finlay and M.A. Lee, Identifying causal effects of reproductive health improvements on women's economic empowerment through the Population Poverty Research Initiative, *The Milbank Quarterly* 96(2), 300–322.

[6] S. Joshi and T.P. Schultz, Family planning and women's and children's health: long-term consequence of an outreach program in Matlab, Bangladesh, *Demography* 50, 149–180 (doi: 10.1007/s13524-012-0172-2).

[7] S. Jayachandran, Social norms as a barrier to women's employment in developing countries (Northwestern University, 2020; JEL codes: O12, J16, J22, Z10).

[8] M. Buvinic, The costs of adolescent childbearing: Evidence from Chile, Barbados, Guatemala, and Mexico, *Studies in Family Planning* 29(2), 201–209 (doi:10.2307/172159).

Finlay underscored that family planning and contraception do influence these trends but precisely *how* family planning influences fertility and women's LFP in low- and middle-income countries could be better understood. She referenced the influential argument by Lant Pritchett[9] that economic development drives down desired fertility, and that this decline leads to a decrease in total fertility rates with or without access to family planning. More recent analysis with greater volumes of data has somewhat supported Pritchett's argument—particularly in sub-Saharan African countries—in that the effect of access to family planning has not overtaken the influence of economic development in declining fertility rates.[10] Finlay indicated that these findings point to other factors that are likely shaping fertility decline, and that more research is needed to identify these factors.

Current studies of the impact of family planning on fertility and women's LFP have produced a patchwork of results that could be contextualized within the framework of long-standing questions about fertility preferences and related declines. Finlay signaled that as the field begins to examine the role of family planning in women's empowerment outcomes, study designs should carefully consider how fertility preferences are shaped by economic development, family planning, and new factors yet to be determined.

During the discussion that followed the presentation, Alex Ezeh (Drexel University) asked whether Finlay had observed any influence of marital status on women's post-childbirth LFP. Finlay replied that marital status crystallizes differences in the relationship between LFP and fertility across continents and income groups. In sub-Saharan African countries, the birth of additional children increases LFP among women in all but the richest income groups. However, in Latin American countries this relationship was observed only in the poorest women, and in South Asian countries it was not observed at all. Finlay explained that variation in income-sharing and lone motherhood may drive these regional differences, and suggested that the effects of marital status on the relationship between LFP and fertility warrant further study. Naila Kabeer (London School of Economics and Political Science) added that women's LFP in South Asian countries has been observed to decline at the point of marriage, whereas in other parts of the world this decreased participation often occurs after the birth of the first child.

Finlay received several questions regarding the nexus between family planning and LFP, including distinctions between organized family planning and general family planning, the influence of employment quality,

---

[9] L.H. Pritchett, Desired fertility and the impact of population policies, *Population and Development Review 20*(1), 1–55.

[10] I. Günther and K. Harttgen, Desired fertility and number of children born across time and space, *Demography 53*(1), 55–83 (doi: 10.1007/s13524-015-0451-9; PMID: 26786205).

and the impacts of birth spacing. She believed that while these questions were important, it was not possible to answer them based on the current peer-reviewed literature. In some cases this difficulty was attributable to a simple need for more time to accommodate the longitudinal studies capable of answering these questions (e.g., the minimum number of years required to study a birth spacing of five years is quite high).

GENDER, LIVELIHOODS, AND AGENCY: TRACKING PATHWAYS OF SOCIAL CHANGE

Naila Kabeer (London School of Economics and Political Science) began by explaining the importance of distinguishing among different domains of women's empowerment, because change does not occur in uniform ways across them. She discussed how access to resources and opportunities translates into immediate and long-term outcomes within these domains and which outcomes allow women to challenge patriarchal structures.

Kabeer situated empowerment as one of three different kinds of agency that are promoted by access to livelihood resources:[11] *capability* (i.e., expanded ways of "being and doing"), *empowerment* (i.e., expanded ways of "being, doing, thinking, feeling, and knowing" that seek to challenge the gender inequalities of daily life), and *citizenship* (i.e., actively engaging in public and political life to promote gender equality or social justice). Empowerment may be viewed as a form of capability that challenges power structures. These power structures, though variable on a global scale, share common features, such as an asymmetrical division of labor between paid and unpaid work among men and women, and norms and ideologies that position women in a lower position of power. While empowerment applies to the individual, citizenship is a form of agency that challenges power structures in a collective manner. Concepts of citizenship can further distinguish between "status" (in other words, the rights afforded to a group of citizens) and "practice" (in other words, actions taken to claim, expand, and renegotiate those rights).

Women's access to resources such as credit and education impact the well-being of children, including their survival rates and their education. Capabilities that fall within this scope lie within women's traditional roles as mothers and wives and enable them to perform those roles, but these capabilities do not necessarily translate to empowerment; however, they *do* translate to empowerment when they are used to diminish gender inequalities and challenge patriarchal power structures.

[11] N. Kabeer, Three faces of agency in feminist economics: capabilities, empowerment, and Citizenship (Ch. 10 in *Handbook of Feminist Economics,* edited by G. Berik and E. Kongar, New York: Routledge, 2020).

In the discussion, Jocelyn Finlay emphasized the significance of Kabeer's comments regarding forms of agency that do not challenge gender inequalities and provided examples from recent work by Erica Field (Duke University) and Rohini Pande (Harvard University). Kabeer said that studies show that women's literacy and LFP in India (when controlling for regional variation in patriarchal structures) are associated with a diminution of the gender gap in mortality as well as an increase in fertility levels, suggesting a degree of strategic agency for women. Kabeer also discussed another study conducted in India that demonstrated an increased investment in the education of girls by mothers who participated in the national employment guarantee scheme, while the participation of fathers in this same scheme had no impact on girls' education and a negative impact on boys' education; thus, male and female access to resources has a ripple effect on the well-being and empowerment of children.

To further evaluate the effects of empowerment on women themselves, Kabeer and colleagues conducted a survey in Ghana, Egypt, and Bangladesh using a common questionnaire that assessed indicators of different domains of empowerment: individual, family, and community.[12] In all three countries, formal employment was more consistently associated with empowerment indicators than informal employment; changes to social norms were often easier to negotiate within a household than within a wider community; and location exerted an influence on empowerment indicators; for example, there was less evidence of change in conservative areas of Egypt and Bangladesh. Kabeer further described how "customary" and "contemporary" resources[13] could have similar outcomes: for example, in Bangladesh, women who were educated and formally employed and women who were religious and dressed conservatively were both consulted by their communities as sources of authority. Kabeer also noted that when economic interventions for women are accompanied by not only material change but also by sources of cognitive change (i.e., changes in how they viewed restrictive norms and practices), sustained evidence of empowerment is more likely.

Citizenship as a form of agency draws attention to rights and deficits of women. It ties agency to the fight for gender justice. Kabeer said that political awareness and agency rarely occur spontaneously among subordinated groups but may require external support. As far as women workers are concerned, their struggles for economic citizenship have not always been

---

[12] N. Kabeer et al., *Paid Work, Women's Empowerment and Inclusive Growth: Transforming the Structures of Constraint* (UN Women Policy Paper, January 2013). Available: http://www.unwomen.org/~/media/headquarters/attachments/sections/library/publications/2013/1/paid-work-womens-empowerment-and-inclusive-growth2%20pdf.pdf.

[13] S.K. Head et al., Customary and contemporary resources for women's empowerment in Bangladesh, *Development in Practice* 25(3), 360-374.

supported by mainstream trade unions. It has often been women's organizations and unions that have taken up their cause. Studies from Latin America found that women workers are more willing to join women's organizations than trade unions, out of solidarity as well as the expectation that a women's organization is more likely to recognize and act on gender-specific discrimination than male-dominated unions. The kinds of organizations working with women matter for outcomes. For instance, women who belonged to associations in Bangladesh experienced a greater impact on empowerment than associations in Ghana and Egypt. The reason for this might be that the associations in Bangladesh were often nongovernmental organizations (NGOs) with some degree of commitment to women's equality, while the associations in Ghana were largely Christian organizations and more interested in women's religious well-being, and the organizations in Egypt were largely state-sponsored and tied to state objectives.

Kabeer said that microfinance and savings groups are among the most studied for evidence of women's empowerment. Kabeer shared her work in Bangladesh, which compared minimalist microfinance with socially-oriented microfinance and social mobilization organizations; the study revealed that minimalist microfinance had neither political nor economic effects, socially oriented microfinance had mixed results, and social mobilization organizations—which organized around savings groups and commitments to change—had the greatest effect on what she called citizenship. These impacts manifested as greater involvement in the public domain, an increased willingness to fight for justice for others, and mobilization against dowries, among other changes.[14] Kabeer also shared evidence from a study in India, which showed the impact of self-help groups on the citizenship and political empowerment of women (e.g., increased voter participation and engagement with local officials) even in the absence of considerable changes in livelihood.[15] Spillover effects on the empowerment of individuals who are not members of the self-help groups have also been observed.

Kabeer also noted that although they take many valuable forms, change and agency do not have equal impacts on patriarchal structures. Furthermore, these changes are not inevitably interrelated and do not display unidirectional causality; while basic capabilities may give rise to individual empowerment, collective action may lead to improvements in basic capabilities, and increases in individual empowerment may build courage to fight for broader social justice.

---

[14] N. Kabeer, Between affiliation and autonomy: navigating pathways of women's empowerment and gender justice in Bangladesh, *Development and Change* 42(2): 499–528.

[15] A. Deshpande and S. Khanna, *Can Weak Ties Create Social Capital? Evidence from Self-Help Groups in India*, Department of Economics Discussion Paper 23 (Ashoka University, 2020).

Amy Tsui (Johns Hopkins University, *emerita*) inquired about the distinction between empowerment and agency, particularly whether the former is a subtype of the latter. Kabeer responded that everyone has some form of agency, or purpose of action; however, the way people use that agency has implications for power relations. Empowerment is therefore a method of using one's agency to challenge manifestations of inequalities in daily life. By way of example, Kabeer noted that some educated women in India will use their agency to discriminate against daughters; while this action may be agency, it reinforces gender discrimination and is therefore not a form of empowerment. In contrast, Kabeer reiterated that increases in literacy and LFP close the gender gaps in survival rates, when controlling for regional patriarchies, across India, which challenges traditional cultural norms and is thus emblematic of empowerment.

Anita Raj (University of California, San Diego) asked Kabeer to elaborate further on the concept of citizenship as agency that is related to a fight for social justice. Kabeer asserted that movement against patriarchal norms takes courage and is often unsustainable when undertaken by a lone individual; for example, a woman who refuses to pay her daughter's dowry may be empowered herself but will not change the institution of dowries. Kabeer then alluded to fellow presenter Seema Jayachandran's (Northwestern University) work, which she said demonstrated the measurable impact of two women working together; when two women expand to a group of women, Kabeer suggested, the likelihood of structural change increases greatly. In this way, citizenship represents a progression of individual empowerment to collective action that challenges patriarchy.

SOCIAL NORMS AS A BARRIER TO FEMALE EMPLOYMENT IN DEVELOPING COUNTRIES

Seema Jayachandran (Northwestern University) discussed the role of social norms as a barrier to female employment and the resulting implications of that barrier for public policy. She noted that this presentation was based on a review article.[16]

A U-shaped relationship exists between a country's economic development and rates of female employment, such that the lowest rates of female employment exist in countries at the middle of the economic development spectrum. Jayachandran explained that this initial drop in female employment as economies develop stems from jobs moving away from the home and from social norms influencing the employment of women in those

[16] S. Jayachandran, *Social Norms as a Barrier to Women's Employment in Developing Countries*. NBER No. w27449 (Cambridge, MA: National Bureau of Economic Research, 2020).

jobs, as well as from the rise of wealthier families that can afford to remove women from the workforce. As economies develop further, structural transformations occur in which more jobs require intellectual rather than physical ability, thereby giving women additional opportunities to re-enter the workforce. Jayachandran used this framework to contextualize the relationship between economic development, female employment, and public policy that aims to accelerate women's ability to participate in service jobs as they emerge in an economy (e.g., through business microcredit or girls' education).

Jayachandran called attention to the large dispersion of countries around the U-shaped curve, such that many countries exist in a state of economic development and female employment that lies well above or below the best-fit line for the data. For example, two countries can have the same gross domestic product but considerably different rates of female employment. Therefore, she argued, policy agendas that will enable women to find employment must account for these sources of variation. Patriarchal gender norms, which also vary throughout the world, are one candidate to explain these differences.

Jayachandran considered many specific norms and noted that they are not restricted to low-income countries; these norms include stigma about women serving as the family breadwinner, restrictions on women's physical mobility and social interactions, acceptability of the harassment of women in public spaces, expectations related to control over household finances, and responsibility for household chores and child care. Jayachandran posited that to close the gap in women's employment between countries, two potential policy approaches may be taken. The first may be to design policies that are *informed* by a country's social norms (i.e., that consider what norms must be circumvented in the design of a program to increase employment), and the second may be to use policy to *change* the norms altogether.

Jayachandran shared an example of one program in Ahmedabad, India, that was designed to work within the social norms of this conservative region—namely, restrictions on women's physical mobility.[17] Jayachandran and colleagues worked with the Self Employed Women's Association, a trade union that works with low-income self-employed women and offers services to increase their business knowledge and opportunities (e.g., by offering microcredit loans). The collaborative project sought to counteract norms concerning physical mobility—which restrict women's peer networks—by allowing women to invite someone to accompany them to a business training program. When women attended the business program alone, they did not make progress in their business development (e.g.,

---

[17] E. Field et al. Friendship at work: can peer effects catalyze female entrepreneurship? *American Economic Journal: Economic Policy* 8(2), 125–153.

women were no more likely to take out loans to expand their business or see increased profits than women who did not attend the training); however, when women attended the program with a friend, they were more likely to take out and repay business loans as well as earn higher business profits.

Interestingly, in that Ahmedabad example the attendance rate did not vary when women could bring a friend, nor did program comprehension seem to differ between the two social conditions. Instead, this result appeared to be driven by more ambitious goal-setting by the women who brought a friend to the program. This difference may very well be related to the norms of restricted mobility, in which women are generally less likely to have a strong network of peers with whom they can travel to business classes and collaborate on business ideas, and Jayachandran said that this case shows how policies and programs need not change a social norm or restriction in order to mitigate it.

Jayachandran shared findings from a second project that did aim to change social norms.[18] In this case, high school students (grades 7–10) in Haryana, India, were exposed to new attitudes toward gender and female employment. (Jayachandran noted that this relatively small-scale project would not change the norms of an entire community, but could do so if scaled up.) Students engaged in sessions (designed by the NGO Breakthrough) that drove reflection on the gender-based norms and restrictions in their society and learned some of the human rights arguments about how those restrictions harm their society. The intervention had a large impact on gender attitudes: 16 percent of regressive attitudes converted to support for gender equality. This effect size remained similar 2.5 years after the program ended, suggesting a persistent attitude change; that persistence was somewhat more long-lasting in boys than girls, reinforcing the need to involve boys in these programs. In addition to attitudes, boys' behavior also seemed to change more than girls' behavior following the program, possibly because their behavior faced fewer constraints. Jayachandran noted that an opportunity exists to increase the scope of this program beyond its original two years and that she hopes to conduct follow-ups with students who completed the program to assess employment rates among the female students and the male students' wives.

Jayachandran concluded her presentation by suggesting that, although traditional policies to improve women's labor market outcomes (e.g., training, microcredit, education) are important, more labor market policies could be developed that specifically operate on social gender norms.

[18] D. Dhar, T. Jain, and S. Jayachandran, *Reshaping Adolescents' Gender Attitudes: Evidence from a School-Based Experiment in India.* Working paper (Northwestern University, 2020).

In the discussion that followed, Sunita Kishor (ICF) asked Jayachandran whether intervening with younger children may have a greater or longer-lasting effect. Jayachandran confirmed this possibility and shared plans to investigate the influence of the same intervention in children ages three to four. Mayra Buvinic asked which specific behaviors were measured in the study. Jayachandran answered that most measures were self-reported attitudes about norm-related behaviors, such as the performance of chores at home. However, the study team also measured increases in completion of a college scholarship application by girls who participated in the program, which it plans to follow up on by examining college attendance among those girls.

Jocelyn Finlay asked Jayachandran whether a current lack of income-sharing in sub-Saharan African households signals a possible divergence from the U-shaped curve of the relationship between women's LFP and a country's economic progress as that region develops. Jayachandran considered it possible that a lack of pooled income would mitigate the traditional decline in women's LFP as sub-Saharan African countries develop further. However, she noted, the structural transformations that lead to jobs moving away from the agricultural sector and toward employment, a move that is more difficult to balance with child-rearing, would likely occur in these countries as well. Jayachandran suggested that it is difficult to predict whether the decrease in women's LFP will manifest in sub-Saharan African countries because the U-shaped curve has also shifted up over time. She likened this shift to what Nancy Birdsall (Center for Global Development) described as a "globalization of norms" or "fixed time effect" as social norms have improved over time. Jayachandran added that these improvements could be driven by increased levels of education among girls.

3

Measuring Women's Empowerment

Points Highlighted by the Presenters

- To measure empowerment, researchers must decide on the level of the measure (e.g., individual, interpersonal, societal); decide how to capture a complex process that includes bargaining, negotiating, and making choices in the face of resistance; and select an appropriate domain of empowerment. (Ushma Upadhyay, University of California, San Francisco)
- Key challenges in measuring empowerment include distinguishing between social norms as attributes of communities versus attributes of individuals; distinguishing between collective and individual agency; distinguishing between empowerment vis-à-vis family members and empowerment in relation to social institutions; and taking account of the fact that both empowerment and family planning are dynamic rather than static processes. (Sonalde Desai, University of Maryland)
- The field lacks a comprehensive measure of women's sexual and reproductive health agency that is consistently defined, operationalized, and validated across groups, contexts, and time. (Kathryn Yount, Emory University)
- Women's preferences need to be understood alongside their self-perceptions and choices to fully understand agency. Goal-setting, sense of agency, and acting on goals, are three dimensions of agency, and need to be analyzed together across contexts. There is also a need to broaden the scope of existing measures across domains and age ranges, and to conduct more systematic adaptation to local contexts. (Aletheia Donald, World Bank)

Mayra Buvinic (United Nations Foundation) served as moderator for this session. She explained that the concept of women's empowerment gained traction during the early 2000s with the work of Amartya Sen and then Naila Kabeer. According to Buvinic, theoretical work focused on concepts related to empowerment dominated the field for more than a decade due to the intrinsic difficulty of *measuring* empowerment. Buvinic said that serious efforts to empirically measure women's empowerment—particularly economic empowerment—have emerged over the past 5 to 6 years.

THE LITERATURE ON THE RELATIONSHIP BETWEEN WOMEN'S EMPOWERMENT AND FERTILITY

In 2014, Ushma Upadhyay (University of California, San Francisco) published a review of the literature on the relationship between women's empowerment and fertility.[1] Among the 60 articles she reviewed, women's empowerment had been measured by 120 different proxy conceptualizations. Upadhyay acknowledged that there are different ways to operationalize the concept of empowerment for research purposes. Researchers must first determine the level of empowerment that they wish to measure: individual, interpersonal, or societal (local/community, regional, or national). On the individual level, she said, measurements usually take the form of indices, such as gender attitudes, that relate to the individual. Interpersonal measurements can quantify a woman's power in relation to others—such as her partner or her health care provider—at a very nuanced level; interpersonal measurements can also characterize family support structures and interspousal differences. At the societal level, empowerment measures can capture phenomena such as rates of voting or child marriage, and in multilevel analyses they can do so alongside individual or interpersonal measures. Upadhyay pointed to a need to perform more varieties of measurements in multiple contexts to interrogate how contextual changes influence individual power.

Empowerment measures must capture a complex process, Upadhyay noted, one that includes bargaining, negotiating, and making choices in the face of resistance. While most studies utilize single-timepoint indicators of empowerment, longitudinal studies encounter the logistical challenge of collecting these indicators over time.

Any selected measure of empowerment also must capture actual choices. Upadhyay emphasized that many people internalize social norms in ways that constrain their choices or face constraints based on available options. For example, evoking the case of activist Malala Yousafzai, Upadhyay argued

[1] U.D. Upadhyay, J.D. Gipson, M. Withers, et al., Women's empowerment and fertility: A review of the literature, *Social Science & Medicine 115*, 111–120.

that measuring empowerment through education may not be appropriate in cases where education entails a threat of extreme violence that renders it an extremely difficult choice to make. Empowerment is therefore most clearly demonstrated by a *relative* exercise of power within a gender-based system of expectations, and can be measured by relative levels of adherence to gender norms. Measures must also reflect the appropriate domain of empowerment for a given study, such as the legal, economic, or reproductive domain. Upadhyay explained that combining domains of empowerment into one measure reduces the predictive validity of that measure and can mask relative empowerment in one domain compared with the others.

In addition to these methodological challenges, Upadhyay identified current gaps in measures and research on empowerment, including a need for more research in low- and middle-income countries. Currently lacking are measures of women in nonmarital and nonheteronormative relationships, unpartnered women, and adolescents and young adults. In addition, more research is needed concerning the impact of declines in fertility and increases in contraceptive use, as well as evaluations of how gender-transformative approaches affect women's empowerment. In Upadhyay's view, the goals of reducing fertility or increasing family planning should not drive motivation to increase women's empowerment; instead, increasing empowerment as a goal in itself as well as promoting reproductive autonomy—with access to safe and legal abortion as a central feature of that autonomy—should serve as primary motivators for research and efforts related to women's empowerment.

Upadhyay introduced the Sexual & Reproductive Empowerment Scale for Adolescents & Young Adults (SRE Scale for AYA), a collaborative effort to consider empowerment as a predictor of desired contraceptive use among adolescents and young adults (ages 15–24). In quotient form, this scale considers individuals who use a contraceptive method that aligns with their preferences in the numerator and individuals who want to use a contraceptive method other than that which they currently use in the denominator; if no contraceptive method is desired, the individual is sorted based upon his or her ability to act accordingly. The 23-item scale was developed between 2015 and 2019 and reflects seven domains of sexual and reproductive empowerment: sexual safety; self-love; sense of future; sexual pleasure; comfort talking with partner; choice of partners, marriage, and children; and parental support. Although the scale was developed in the United States, Upadhyay hopes to see the scale adapted and tested internationally. Finally, Upadhyay introduced a new resource for women's empowerment measures, the University of California Global Health Institute (UCGHI) Database of Gender and Women's Empowerment Measures.[2]

[2] See http://www.empowermentmeasures.org.

During the discussion that followed the presentation, Alex Ezeh asked why outcomes related to women's fertility and family planning were used to validate the SRE Scale for AYA despite Upadhyay's position that these should not be the ultimate outcomes in measurement of women's empowerment. Upadhyay noted that the validation measure for the SRE Scale for AYA was not contraceptive use but *desired* contraceptive use, which she believes reflects the ultimate goal of reproductive autonomy. The links between women's empowerment, contraceptive use, and fertility reduction are well established in the literature, but if these are the primary motivations for work on women's empowerment, the goal of reproductive autonomy may be overlooked.

Aletheia Donald (World Bank) asked about the degree of overlap between the UCGHI Database of Gender and Women's Empowerment Measures and the EMERGE database.[3] Upadhyay explained that the former focuses on empowerment measures that have been used to assess health outcomes.

Sarah Baird (George Washington University) requested advice on what actions researchers could take when social norms pose challenges to asking a particular survey question. Upadhyay advised that surveys avoid language that marginalizes some respondents. Surveys may also combine encompassing and clarifying language so that questions are understood by the majority. For example, the primary language of a question may use the term "partner" and follow it with a clarifier for those who may not understand this language to refer to their "husband" or "wife."

MEASURING WOMEN'S EMPOWERMENT IN THE CONTEXT OF FAMILY PLANNING

Sonalde Desai (University of Maryland) presented three domains of measurement that describe women's empowerment in family planning and other outcomes. The first domain is *institutional*, in which measurements describe the structure that governs women's agency and interactions. Here Desai drew a distinction between formal institutions (e.g., laws, labor markets, education systems, health services, transportation) and informal institutions (e.g., social norms, stratification systems). The second domain of measurement involves *agency* itself, which can be classified as individual agency (e.g., psychological, social, material, cognitive) or collective agency (e.g., organization, representation, social support, knowledge transfer). The third domain measures *interactions*, such as negotiations with partners and

[3] EMERGE, which stands for Evidence-based Measures of Empowerment for Research on Gender Equality, is a project of the Center on Gender Equity and Health (GEH) at the University of California, San Diego.

family as well as health care providers and bureaucrats. Desai described these domains as micro- and macro-level "building blocks" to consider when measuring empowerment.

Desai said that most literature to date focuses on individual-level agency or intra-family negotiations, partly due to the simple fact that relevant data exist, for example from demographic and health surveys. More recent efforts to expand these measurements attempt to evaluate more dimensions of agency, such as self-efficacy and gender attitudes, and the linkages between social institutions and individual agency, such as through access to paid work, land ownership, and financial inclusion. Desai pointed out that several of the "building blocks" to measure empowerment remain missing, including those that focus on informal institutions, collective agency, interactions with service providers, as well as the influence of changes and interactions over the life course that ultimately lead to increases in agency; these gaps were the focus of Desai's presentation.

A key challenge in measuring informal institutions (such as norms) is the question of whether empowerment varies more among individuals or communities. Desai discussed a study of five Asian countries that demonstrated far greater variation on almost all measures of empowerment among communities than among individuals within a community: 40 to 80 percent of intercommunity variation in empowerment measures (e.g., decision-making ability, freedom of movement, domestic violence) could be explained by aggregated community responses without including any individual traits (e.g., individual educational attainment).[4] She cited the study author's conclusion that the results were "consistent with the assumption that empowerment is a group-based [rather than individual] process."

However, Desai noted that aggregation of data is not especially satisfactory because it may identify spurious relationships. For example, she said that one could posit an effect in which the marital status of her neighbors in graduate school had influenced her own marital status at the time, whereas the fact that she lived in married student housing actually explained that similarity. Thus, measurement of informal institutions must consider whether an attribute describes an individual or a community. For illustrative purposes, Desai provided examples of how surveys might word questions about social norms to capture this distinction between individual gender attitudes and community-based gender norms:

- Measures individual attitudes: "In your opinion, is a husband justified in hitting or beating his wife in the following situations…."

[4] K.O. Mason and H.L. Smith, Husbands' versus wives' fertility goals and use of contraception: the influence of gender context in five Asian countries, *Demography* 37(3), 299–311 (PMID: 10953805).

- Measures community norms: "How many people in your community would think it normal for a man to beat his wife in the following situations...."
- Measures community norms: "If a man failed to punish his wife in the following situations, he would lose respect in your community...."

When measuring agency, it is critical to assess *whose* agency is being measured: the individual's or the collective's. Desai pointed to a body of work that measures individual agency (e.g., self-efficacy, intrahousehold decision-making power, physical mobility), but noted that some situations may call for measures of collective agency. Participation in self-help groups, community involvement in hiring health care workers, informal social networks for discussion of childbearing and contraception, and community-focused sex-education programs are all relevant measures of collective agency for family planning research. Desai pointed out that collective agency is an especially suitable arena for policy intervention.

Desai explained that measurements of social interactions must consider the locus of power in the interaction, for example whether power is exercised vis-à-vis family members or institutions. Measures of empowerment tend to focus on intrahousehold negotiations, yet these interactions may not play a large role in outcome measures. Women and men largely agree on fertility preferences, for example, rendering intrahousehold negotiations less consequential than interactions with health systems.[5] Desai noted that many women in India opt for sterilization over intrauterine devices (IUDs) or birth control pills because health providers emphasize the former practice over the latter, and thus family planning research on this issue should focus on the power imbalance between women and these institutions, not on that between women and their male partners. Data on resistance to or general understanding of overtly or subtly coercive family planning policies can also shed light on women's empowerment, because women with more agency may be better equipped to navigate these systems. Examples of such resistance include subversion of the one-child norm in China and negotiation of provider resistance to offering abortion.

To measure the influence of interactions on women's agency over time, data on stability versus change are needed. Desai explained that empowerment and family planning are dynamic processes and that excessive reliance on cross-sectional data creates a false sense of empowerment as a stable attribute of individuals. Although work exists on LFP and fertility over time, longitudinal data on other aspects of gender empowerment will enable

[5] K.O. Mason and H.L. Smith, Husbands' versus wives' fertility goals and use of contraception: the influence of gender context in five Asian countries, *Demography* 37(3), 299–311 (PMID: 10953805).

family planning research in more areas, including growth in intrahousehold power following the birth of a son in patriarchal societies, the ability to continue paid work with longer birth spacing, childcare constraints on community participation, and the identification of key ages or life stages where family planning interventions matter most. Desai emphasized that the field may be able to understand only some of these dynamic relationships through the collection and analysis of longitudinal data. Finally, she concluded by acknowledging that variation among countries and cultures, as well as intra-country variation (e.g., intersectionality by race, gender, class), were not addressed in this presentation despite their importance.

Following Desai's presentation, Mayra Buvinic called upon funding agencies to prioritize longitudinal studies of women's empowerment and family planning. Sajeda Amin (Population Council) asked whether complications with data aggregation can be addressed through strategic study design and the use of the level of aggregation as a reference group. Desai responded by highlighting two potential issues specifically related to aggregating data from the reference group of neighbors. First, spurious relationships in the data may be generated, which Desai acknowledged can be rectified through strategic research design. Second, social norms may not be reflected in the behavior of neighbors; for example, even if norms dictate that women working outside the home is a sign of low status, no one in a poor neighborhood could live up to that norm even though they subscribed to it.

Jocelyn Finlay inquired whether the research community can press the Demographic and Health Surveys (DHS) Program to embrace longitudinal studies. Desai advocated for more longitudinal research in general but also explained that it may not be easily achieved in large, cross-national data sets. Sunita Kishor added that DHS cannot tackle every methodological problem and that a push for longitudinal DHS studies is aspirational. Kishor also said that longitudinal data will likely be more useful when focused on a specific set of key indicators, and noted that donors and survey funders are interested in innovative survey designs that might allow for a subset of longitudinal measures.

Nancy Birdsall inquired whether anyone on the panel had leveraged natural experiments to measure women's empowerment. Desai shared that three natural experiments occurred between two survey waves in India: first, the implementation of a job guarantee program that had a positive impact on women's LFP; second, the introduction of cash transfers for hospital deliveries, which also had a positive impact on women's LFP; and third, the introduction of transportation networks within a village, which led to women's participation in nonagricultural work. Birdsall added that another critical opportunity for a natural experiment would be to follow a policy change specifically related to contraception access, family planning, or general reproductive health.

MEASURING WOMEN'S AGENCY IN FAMILY PLANNING RESEARCH: A CALL TO TRANSFORM PARADIGMS

Kathryn M. Yount (Emory University) described a process to conceptualize and measure agency, with emphasis on the fact that although agency may be an abstract concept, it is nonetheless important to define it as a validated multidimensional construct that can be applied consistently across contexts.

Yount presented findings from a literature review that evaluated the relationship between measures of women's agency and contraceptive use in low- and middle-income countries.[6] This review spanned multiple decades and languages, and focused on quantitative analyses of population-based surveys that narrowly defined agency as freedom of movement and decision-making. The review was restricted to 12 studies that met the inclusion criteria; these studies were conducted between 1996 and 2014, primarily in sub-Saharan African and South Asian low- and middle-income countries, and generally relied on DHS data. Yount described the quality of the included studies as either low or moderate, and highlighted the various ways that researchers referred to empowerment and contraceptive use as well as the ways they inconsistently applied or vaguely defined measures. Given this considerable variability in clearly defined, operationalized constructs in the literature, it was unsurprising to Yount and colleagues that the relationships identified among measures of decision-making, freedom of movement, and contraceptive use were mixed. One study, however, was conducted in a sub-Saharan low- or middle-income country and relied on more items of measurement, two latent constructs, and specific measures of contraceptive use; this study did find a positive relationship between both aspects of agency and contraceptive use.[7]

Yount then presented a sampling of measures of women's sexual and reproductive health (SRH) agency. Rather than offering a comprehensive measure of women's overall SRH agency, these measures tend to focus on specific concepts, such as sexual activity, HIV risk, prevention of pregnancy using contraception, adolescent SRH, and agency in pregnancy. They vary substantially in dimensionality, item number, level of validation, and method of psychometric assessment. In addition, few studies have evaluated these measures with regard to test-retest reliability or replicated

[6] L. James-Hawkins, C. Peters, K. VanderEnde, L. Bardin, K.M. Yount, Women's agency and its relationship to current contraceptive use in lower- and middle-income countries: a systematic review of the literature, *Global Public Health 13*(7), 843–858 (doi: 10.1080/17441692.2016.1239270; Epub 2016 Oct 1. PMID: 27690750).

[7] M. Corroon, I.S. Speizer, J.C. Fotso, et al. The role of gender empowerment on reproductive health outcomes in urban Nigeria, *Maternal and Child Health Journal 18*(1), 307–315 (doi:10.1007/s10995-013-1266-1).

cross-cultural validation, which is a concern for longitudinal research that tracks agency over time. Yount asserted that the field currently lacks a comprehensive measure of women's SRH agency that is consistently defined, operationalized, and validated across groups, context, and time.

Yount offered a multidimensional construct of agency defined as a process of conscientization whereby women—individually and collectively—become aware of and act to overcome their disempowerment. The three dimensions of this construct are *intrinsic agency, instrumental agency,* and *collective agency*. Intrinsic agency includes state of mind, awareness of rights and aspirations, confidence in capabilities, and internal motivation to act. Instrumental agency includes acting strategically, exercising voice, influencing decisions, and moving freely in historically restricted spaces. Collective agency includes connection, joint efficacy, engaging in or leading networks with shared goals, and joint action in pursuit of shared goals to effect change.

In addition, Yount and colleagues have designed a sequential, mixed-methods process to develop scales of women's agency that are both general and specific to SRH. Steps in this process include qualitative research; questionnaire review; item pool development; expert review to assess the item pool; cognitive testing with target populations and critical stakeholders; form pretesting; pilot survey; psychometric validation; and replication across groups, contexts, and time. This process can identify comparable measures of women's agency and validated contextual items, although Yount emphasized that skipping any of these steps could compromise the resulting scale.

Given the variation in methods used in the field, Yount reviewed the specific steps taken to perform the psychometric validation phase of this process. These steps include univariate and bivariate analysis of included items; exploratory factor analysis in a random-split sample to assess dimensionality; confirmatory factor analysis in a second random-split sample; and measurement invariance analysis across groups, across contexts, and over time. After generating a valid, long-form measure of women's agency, short-form subsets of measures may be identified that are adequate when less time is available to survey.

Yount provided two examples of measures recently validated by the proposed construct definition and development process: the Women's Agency Scale 61 (WAS-61),[8] a general agency measure composed of 61 validated items tightly linked to dimensions of intrinsic, instrumental, and collective agency; and the Reproductive Agency Scale 17 (RAS-17[9]), a

[8] K.M. Yount, Z. Khan, S. Miedema, Y. F. Cheong, and R. T. Naved, *The Women's Agency Scale 61 (Was-61): a Comprehensive Measure of Women's Intrinsic, Instrumental, and Collective Agency* (available at SSRN).

[9] K.M. Yount, L. James-Hawkins, and H.F.A. Rahim, The Reproductive Agency Scale (RAS-17): development and validation in a cross-sectional study of pregnant Qatari and non-Qatari Arab Women, *BMC Pregnancy and Childbirth 20*(1), 1–15.

more concise measure of reproductive health agency developed in Qatar that consists of 17 items that are also linked to the aforementioned three key dimensions of agency. Yount concluded that if the field can agree on a set of concepts that focus on intrinsic, instrumental, and collective agency, then the development of consistent and widely applicable general and SRH agency measures is achievable.

During the discussion, Yount added that in conducting a survey experiment in Bangladesh, her team has found that responses are sensitive to changes in question wording and order and that it is important to bring rigor to the measurement of agency in this regard. Amy Tsui asked whether any panelist had experience measuring change in empowerment at the community level in a randomized experiment. Yount responded that Emory University is collaborating with CARE on a large community-based randomized trial that will assess a social-norm-change initiative and a movement-building initiative among adolescent girls. The trial will have the capacity to measure intergenerational and community-level changes in intrinsic, instrumental, and collective agency.

MEASURING WOMEN'S AGENCY

Aletheia Donald (World Bank) described agency as a central component that binds resources to outcomes, such as child nutritional status and contraceptive use, and emphasized the importance of measuring empowerment consistently in order to definitively characterize this relationship. Citing Naila Kabeer's definition of agency, Donald explained that agency is the "ability to define one's goals and act on them" and further outlined three required dimensions of this ability: goal-setting, perceived control and ability ("sense of agency"), and acting on goals.[10]

In order to understand an individual's ability to set goals (the first dimension of agency), one must assess the individual's capacity to define goals as well as to align those goals with the individual's own values and preferences. Goal-setting is often measured by standardized questionnaires and scales in industrial and organizational psychology research, and in the context of entrepreneurial interventions in Africa it is often measured by post-coding respondents' goals based on specificity and detail.[11] Donald noted that questions about goals and preferences have more recently been used to complement questions about decision-making roles in recognition

[10] N. Kabeer, Resources, agency, and achievements: reflections on the measurement of women's empowerment, *Development and Change 30*(3), 435–464.

[11] M. Frese, S. Krauss, N. Keith, S. Escher, et al., Business owners' action planning and its relationship to business success in three African countries, *The Journal of Applied Psychology* 92, 1481–1498 (doi: 10.1037/0021-9010.92.6.1481).

of the fact that a woman's desire to make a decision is a critical factor in assessing whether her involvement in that decision truly reflects agency. The most common measure of whether an individual's goals align with her (or his) values is the Relative Autonomy Index.[12] This index measures the extent to which motivation is external (e.g., a product of coercion or avoiding repercussions), introjected (i.e., to adhere to norms), or identified (i.e., an autonomous preference). Work in this area typically utilizes hypothetical vignettes to ground respondents' answers.

Individuals' "sense of agency" (the second dimension of agency) has been studied in many disciplines. Measurement of this sense of control in cognitive science has employed brain imaging studies and sensory tests that capture different perceptions of self- and externally generated stimuli. The social sciences have historically conceptualized sense of agency according to a framework developed by Ellen Skinner in the 1990s, which characterizes the relationship between resources, or means, and goal-related outcomes, or ends. Donald outlined two prominent concepts related to this framework: *locus of control* and *self-efficacy*. Locus of control is the degree to which one believes an event is caused by one's own actions, while self-efficacy is the belief in one's capability to bring about an action. Locus of control is traditionally measured using the Rotter I-E Scale, which distinguishes between external and internal loci of control, or the Multidimensional IPC (Internality/Powerful Others/Chance) Scale, which further parses external locus of control according to an individual's belief that an outcome is a function of chance or the will of a powerful "other." Both scales have been validated for well-educated professional sub-populations, and Donald noted their increasing use among low-literacy populations. Self-efficacy has been measured as both generalized and domain-specific self-efficacy; Donald pointed to the Condom Use Self-Efficacy Scale as a validated example, which has been used in Ghana to evaluate one's efficacy to use condoms or negotiate the use of condoms with partners.

Donald said that because scales that measure sense of agency can be quite long, some measurements have been developed that attempt to describe the "means-ends" relationship directly. The most popular is the Control Scale, in which respondents grade their perceived sense of control over the direction and outcome of their lives on a scale of 1 to 10; internationally, women score significantly lower than men on the Control Scale. The Fate Scale, which is more closely related to locus of control, was introduced more recently and asks respondents to grade their belief that they control their destiny on a scale of 1 to 10. The World Value Survey

[12] R.M. Ryan and E.L. Deci, Self-determination theory and the facilitation of intrinsic motivation, social development, and well-being, *American Psychologist* 55(1), 68–78 (doi: 10.1037/0003-066X.55.1.68).

collected nationally representative data from 90 countries for both the Control and Fate Scales and demonstrated that response discrepancies vary systematically across income levels; the responses to both scales overlap nearly perfectly in high-income countries, and the discrepancy between responses becomes progressively larger with lower income levels. This relationship between income level and response discrepancy also differs by gender. Indeed, Donald pointed out that the only region where the response discrepancy is small and similar across genders is North America. Donald warned that researchers must take care when conducting cross-country analyses to consider the systematic influence of poverty and gender on outcome measurements.

The capacity to act on goals (the third dimension of agency) has been measured since the 1960s through surveys of intrahousehold decision-making roles.[13] Donald highlighted two main drawbacks to the most commonly-used decision-making questions: first, the questions fail to capture negotiations or bargaining processes as they relate to decision-making in a household, and second, ambiguous phrasing can lead to varied interpretation of questions by respondents in ways that are systematic and exceed random measurement error. Some measures, including the Women's Empowerment in Agriculture Index, aim to address the weaknesses in these surveys by asking questions specifically related to decision-making processes, such as "How much input do you have in making decisions about a certain topic?" or "To what extent do you feel you can make your own decisions if you want to?"

About 11 years ago, the DHS started to separately ask husbands and wives questions about household decision-making roles. Donald presented results from a study that analyzed these data from more than 71,000 couples across 23 sub-Saharan African countries, focusing on questions about decision-making roles for major household purchases.[14] Consistent with previous public health research, the study showed that well-being outcomes, such as those concerning women's general and reproductive health, are often highest when spouses agree on the woman's power, yet nearly half of couples disagreed about roles and decision-making power.

Compared to cases of uncontested power or of husbands "giving" power, cases of women "taking" power were more positively correlated with key economic empowerment proxies (e.g., higher earnings than their husbands, land ownership). Women "taking" power was more strongly

[13] R.O. Blood, Jr., and D.M. Wolfe, *Husbands and Wives: The Dynamics of Family Living* (Free Press Glencoe, 1960).

[14] J. Annan, A. Donald, M. Goldstein, P. Gonzalez Martinez, and G. Koolwal, *Taking Power: Women's Empowerment and Household Well-Being in Sub-Saharan Africa*, Policy Research Working Paper No. 9034 (Washington, DC: World Bank, 2019 (https://openknowledge.worldbank.org/handle/10986/32494).

related to beneficial household welfare outcomes (e.g., children's health, women's reproductive health) than husbands "giving" power. In some cases, women "taking" power was even associated with similar benefits as them having uncontested power, such as for girls' stunting and wasting, or an increased prevalence of outcomes such as women terminating a pregnancy. However, Donald also noted a stark relationship between women "taking" power and higher prevalence of emotional violence. Donald said that analysis of response discrepancy is an active field, and that what may at first seem like unreliable self-report data can actually provide insight into different aspects of women's agency.

Donald called for more systematic analytical work to test alternative forms of measurement and the appropriateness of measurements in the context of given policy circumstances and research questions. Some of this research should evaluate all three dimensions of agency together across contexts in order to consider women's preferences alongside self-perceptions and to provide a more comprehensive understanding of agency. She also recommended that measurements of agency be expanded to include other age groups and designed to systematically adapt to local contexts. A new collaboration called Measures for Advancing Gender Equality (MAGNET) aims to fill some of the existing gaps. Donald noted that advances in agency measurement will help sharpen theoretical insights on how households actually work, and lead to the design of better programs and policies that can more effectively target particular cognitive or behavioral pathways in enhancing women's empowerment.

In the discussion, Anita Raj asked for examples of advancements in the measurement of self-efficacy and decision making. Donald replied that scales for measuring self-efficacy have been introduced in contexts where they were not previously used, such as in entrepreneurship impact evaluations. For measures of decision-making, questions have increasingly been designed to unpack the process that generated the final decision, such as a woman's sense of input and her decisional outcomes in the event of conflict. They have also moved toward analyzing dimensions of agency, such as by assessing decision making alongside measures of motivational autonomy or locus of control.

Kathryn Yount added that labor force panel surveys in Egypt and Jordan contain longitudinal data on decision-making, attitudes about violence, and freedom of movement that show a subset of items that are time-invariant over a 12-year period, indicating a capacity to develop indices that can track change over time. Yount also commented that there is a tendency to include general self-efficacy measures when assessing women's agency and advocated for making those general measures more specific (e.g., confidence in self-expression, confidence in influencing decisions).

4

Ways of Addressing Current Data Limitations

Points Highlighted by the Presenters

- Shocks such as the COVID-19 pandemic can produce substantial shifts in household dynamics and can influence women's empowerment. New measurement and analysis of data from long-running studies can detect these shifts. (Philip Anglewicz, Johns Hopkins University)
- Constructs and measures used in family research that are currently performing well include agency, response to agency, and family planning stigma/rights. Promising measures that need strengthening include those relating to social norms and quality of care in family planning. Critical gaps in measurement persist for agency in fertility, contraceptive discontinuation, ambivalence/not planning, forms of resistance (e.g., covert use), sexuality/pleasure, and critical consciousness and choice. (Anita Raj, University of California, San Diego)
- Empowerment is by definition a process, and this creates a need for longitudinal studies and data on empowerment for different stages of the life course. More qualitative data are also needed to assist in interpreting the survey data that are collected. (Sunita Kishor, ICF)

Nancy Birdsall (Center for Global Development) served as moderator for this session. She began by underscoring how much the discourse on population and family planning issues has evolved since the 1970s. Birdsall said that this session would set a standard for future research on these topics based on better data—perhaps of a longitudinal, collective-level, or aggregate nature.

WOMEN'S ECONOMIC EMPOWERMENT AND COVID-19: RESULTS FROM PERFORMANCE MONITORING FOR ACTION

Philip Anglewicz (Johns Hopkins University) noted that shocks, such as climate disasters or pandemics, have a profound impact on people's health, well-being, and economic status. Shocks also change household bargaining dynamics and may influence women's economic empowerment. The COVID-19 pandemic is a prime example of a shock with the potential to influence these dynamics. Anglewicz provided background on the COVID-19 pandemic in sub-Saharan Africa, where more than 1 million confirmed cases and more than 23,000 deaths were reported by mid-August. Many regional governments quickly enacted travel bans, mobility restrictions, limitations on public gatherings, and other measures to prevent the spread of COVID-19; consequently, greater than 75 percent of households monitored by the Performance Monitoring for Action (PMA) project lost at least some portion of their income, while 30 percent lost all income. The PMA project has been adapted to leverage previous and future waves of data collection to explore the impact of the COVID-19 shock.

PMA operates in eight countries: Burkina Faso, Côte d'Ivoire, Democratic Republic of the Congo (DRC), India, Kenya, Niger, Nigeria, and Uganda (Anglewicz notes that a PMA project unrelated to this presentation is also under way in Ethiopia). The PMA project in these countries recently shifted from monitoring by repeat cross-section to using a longitudinal-panel design, in which the same women are monitored and interviewed over time in three waves, between 2019 and 2022. During June and July of 2020, a phone survey was conducted on the topic of COVID-19 in four countries for which baseline data had already been collected: Burkina Faso, DRC, Kenya, and Nigeria. This phone survey measured COVID-19 awareness, media exposure, risk perception, knowledge, behavior change, and socioeconomic impact, as well as the disease's impact on family planning, contraceptive use, and fertility intentions. Interviewers remained constant across waves when possible, and responses were recorded on smartphones via Open Data Kit. The Kenya and Burkina Faso samples are nationally representative, while the DRC sample is restricted to Kinshasa and the Nigerian sample is representative of Kano and Lagos states (although only data from Lagos are analyzed here). Follow-up response rates were high in all samples (74.7 to 93.9%).

Anglewicz focused on a commonly used measure of household decision-making to examine women's economic empowerment in these samples over time and after the emergence of COVID-19. The same question was posed to respondents on both the baseline and follow-up survey: "Who usually makes decisions about making household purchases for daily needs: you, your husband/partner, you and your husband/partner jointly, or someone else?" Multinomial logistic regression was performed to analyze characteristics associated with changes in decision-making roles, with a focus on women who made decisions at baseline and assessing the degree of change in that role; characteristics included in the analysis were modern contraceptive use, parity, age, education, household size, wealth tertile, job participation in the previous seven days, and household economic impact of COVID-19.

The analysis revealed that the percentage of households in which women were the decision-makers shrank from baseline to follow-up across the samples, while partner or external decision-making rose. Anglewicz shared results from additional analyses based on who made household decisions at baseline to interrogate the stability of these decision-making relationships and impacts of COVID-19. In households where women made decisions at baseline, approximately one-quarter of those women retained that role in Kenya, Burkina Faso, and Nigeria; when the role did change, it was more likely to shift toward joint decision-making than external or partner decision-making. Women's decision-making was more stable in DRC, where more than one-half of the women retained their role as the primary decision-maker after the pandemic began; however, when roles did change it was more likely to shift toward partner or external decision-making than a joint process.

In Kenya and Burkina Faso, the decision-making role was more stable at follow-up among households in which decisions were made externally by a partner or someone else at baseline than among those in which women made decisions at baseline; when the roles did change, decision-making was more likely to become a joint process than to shift to the woman. In DRC, however, the most frequent scenario at follow-up in these households was for external or partner decision-making to shift to the woman entirely. Joint decision-making was the most stable scenario from baseline to follow-up; if roles changed in these households they were more likely to shift toward partner or external decision-making in Kenya, Burkina Faso, and Nigeria, and were equally likely to shift toward the woman or a partner in DRC.

The analysis also revealed some characteristic patterns related to decision-making dynamics across countries. For example, older women (ages 25–49) were more likely to retain decision-making power than younger women (ages 15–24). In addition, in households that experienced complete or partial income loss following the emergence of COVID-19, decision-making was more likely to shift to a joint process in Burkina Faso and to partner or external power in DRC. In Kenya and Burkina Faso, larger households were more likely to shift away from women holding decision-making power from baseline to follow-up.

These data highlight a fair amount of change in household decision-making power as a result of COVID-19, in which the overall pattern indicates a shift away from women making decisions about daily purchases and toward a joint decision-making process, or toward decision-making by the husband or other household member. Joint decision-making appears to be the scenario experiencing the least change from baseline, while women making decisions by themselves is the most vulnerable to change over time, with teens and young adults experiencing the most change. Anglewicz said that the next measure to be analyzed from the PMA survey assesses whether women's economic reliance on husbands or partners has increased following the implementation of COVID-19 restrictions in their countries. Analyses will also be stratified by baseline wealth quintile and COVID-19 economic impact, and community-level measures of economic development, financial literacy or resources, and women's employment will be added.

Anglewicz said that these COVID-19 data represent only one piece of the intended output from the PMA research. The broad range of women's economic empowerment measures collected at baseline encompasses numerous indicators of economic advancement, power, and agency and will be linked to data from future collection timepoints to produce a longitudinal view of the landscape of women's economic empowerment in these countries. After the second wave of data has been collected, the data will be used to evaluate causal relationships between contraceptive use and women's economic empowerment, as well as the factors that predict which women will gain or lose empowerment over time.

In the discussion, Anglewicz received several questions pertaining to the phone-based survey mode of the PMA study. Aletheia Donald inquired whether the study tracked whether the call was private or on speaker phone when women were contacted for the follow-up survey. Anglewicz clarified that women were asked at the onset to not use a speaker phone and to try to find a place to respond to the survey privately. Alex Ezeh asked how the change in survey mode from in-person (baseline) to phone (follow-up) may have affected the observed changes. To this point, Anglewicz responded that in most cases the surveys were conducted by the same interviewer at baseline and at follow-up to establish a rapport between the questioner and the respondent and to yield better quality data despite the change in survey mode. Furthermore, the influence of using phones as a survey mode was specifically assessed in other data collected in Burkina Faso, and results suggested that the use of phone surveys did not have a large impact on responses of interest to PMA.

Win Brown (Bill & Melinda Gates Foundation) commented that a methodological challenge in this study is the possibility of selection bias due to characteristics associated with phone ownership and the potential need to apply sampling weights accordingly. Anglewicz acknowledged that PMA addressed this challenge by using inverse probability weighting. In this method, the inverse of a score based on the estimated likelihood of women owning a phone (based on certain characteristics) is used to generate a weight, which is then aggregated with weights designed to account for sampling and nonresponse bias. Anglewicz likened the procedure to propensity score matching. After weights were applied, the distributions of sociodemographic characteristics between the weighted and baseline samples were compared to confirm that the weights were effective. As a caveat, Anglewicz noted that women who do not own phones are systematically different from women who do own phones in ways that may be unobservable and unaccounted for by weighting methods. However, based on observed characteristics, it appears that this adjustment was successful in limiting bias.

Anita Raj noted the difficulty in interpreting responses to questions about decision-making and asked whether either joint decision-making or women's unilateral decision-making is better than the other. Anglewicz responded that the answer is likely context-dependent and that more data—particularly longitudinal data that include outcome measures—are needed.

Raj also asked how the researchers can be sure that the observed changes were due to a COVID-19-associated shock rather than a testing effect or other factor. Anglewicz said that the next wave of data will shed light on this question. In addition, data on economic impact intensity and fear of COVID-19 infection can be used to assess overall COVID-19 impact, and PMA plans to analyze variation in changes over time for associations with COVID-19 impact.

Jocelyn Finlay suggested that the intersection of domestic violence outcomes and decision-making would be an interesting dimension to add to this study. Anglewicz responded that domestic violence was not addressed at baseline but that PMA will add a domestic violence module to upcoming survey waves.

MEASURING GENDER EQUITY IN FAMILY PLANNING: LEARNINGS, EXPERIENCES, AND THE WAY FORWARD

Anita Raj (University of California, San Diego) presented an overview of how gender equity measures are used in the context of family planning by the project known as EMERGE (Evidence-based Measures of Empowerment for Research on Gender Equality). The EMERGE Family Planning Project operates under the umbrella of the EMERGE Project, which examines measures used in gender equality and empowerment research more broadly. Its goals were threefold: to identify constructs and measures of agency and norms that are currently used in family planning research, to evaluate the quality of these measures, and to determine outstanding needs in the field.

The EMERGE Family Planning Project has three phases. In Phase 1, which was performed in January 2020, key informant interviews were conducted with SRH experts (n=40) who had developed and operationalized measures for family planning research. In Phase 2, completed in July 2020, a literature review was performed to assess measures from 152 papers across multiple disciplines for psychometrics, cross-national validation, and ease of use. Raj noted that a white paper was produced based on Phases 1 and 2, and that people interested in learning more about the methodologies of this work can find information in that publication.[1] In Phase 3, a conference of experts in the field was held on September 9, 2020, to discuss the results of Phases 1 and 2, as well as future directions for the field; Raj remarked that several speakers at this Virtual Workshop were present at that conference and that the conference will lead to a position paper.

The EMERGE Family Planning Project employed an empowerment framework influenced by psychology, sociology, and political science to conceptualize family planning goals and used measurement constructs that focused on norms, choice, and agency. Raj emphasized that empowerment is a process that pushes against power structures and is rooted in self-determined action, such that actions are empowered as long as they align with the values and preferences of the person performing the actions and especially if they challenge the norm. To this end, Raj cautioned that researchers must be cognizant of the fact that family planning has roots in population control and eugenics, lest the field slip backwards into this dangerous territory by being overly prescriptive regarding what people's choices "should" be.

The project identified several measures of agency that perform well in family planning research, including measures related to contraceptive self-efficacy, sexual communication self-efficacy, and reproductive decision-making autonomy. Raj highlighted that decision-making measures that capture nuances of the decision-making process, such as a woman's desire to make a decision or what happens when disagreements occur, are newer and provide more clarity about women's agency in decision-making. Other high-performing measures currently in use include those that assess response to agency (e.g., male engagement in family planning communication, reproductive coercion) and those that assess family planning stigma

---

[1] N. Bhan, E. Thomas, A. Dixit, et al., *Measuring Women's Agency and Gender Norms in Family Planning: What do we know and where do we go?* (EMERGE [Evidence-based Measures of Empowerment for Research on Gender Equality], Center on Gender Equity and Health, 2020).

or rights (e.g., concerning abortion, adolescent SRH). All of these helpful measures tend to be brief measures that are used in cross-national contexts.

Raj introduced several measures that are promising but need strengthening. Often these measures are in early stages of testing or have been used in single-nation contexts, but they are nevertheless psychometrically rigorous. These promising measures are most commonly related to social norms and quality of care in family planning counseling. Social norm measures include measures of gender norms, male engagement in family planning norms, family or community engagement in FP norms, and fertility and contraceptive use norms. Measures of quality of care in family planning counseling include provider respect, coercion, and effects of incentives or targets on provider behaviors. Raj acknowledged that family planning providers—who are often women—who engage in disrespectful or coercive care are commonly bullied or themselves less respected, which itself is an important area of study.

Critical gaps in family planning research measurements were also identified in the EMERGE Family Planning Project. Measures of agency in fertility were among these gaps, because these measures often focus on agency in contraceptive use but fail to capture agency in reproduction. Contraceptive discontinuation measures appear to lack the nuance required to assess ambivalence or lack of planning. Measures that illustrate forms of resistance (e.g., covert use of contraception), sexuality for pleasure, and critical consciousness and choice (i.e., attributes of choice) were also described by Raj as underdeveloped or lacking in the family planning field. Experts consulted by the EMERGE Family Planning Project pointed to agency in relation to fertility and mistreatment or pressure in services as two of the highest-priority gaps to address in the realm of family planning measures. Raj ended by underscoring that the project suggested to her that there was a consensus in the field concerning what family planning is, namely that it is not contraception, and that the two terms must not be used interchangeably. In addition, Raj stated that empowerment should be the fundamental lens through which the entire community understands family planning in order to improve research surveys and measures.

In the discussion, Jocelyn Finlay asked whether the term "family planning" is even necessary, noting its unhelpfulness for adolescents and youths and for women who are ambivalent on the subject of family planning. Raj replied that this question arose during the September conference of the EMERGE Family Planning Project and that experts in the field support retiring use of the term "family planning." However, Raj noted that it is challenging to change widely understood terminology, and she reiterated her desire to, at a minimum, see an end to the use of the term as synonymous with contraceptive use.

THE DEMOGRAPHIC AND HEALTH SURVEYS: DATA, GAPS, AND SOME THOUGHTS

Sunita Kishor (ICF) explained that the Demographic and Health Surveys (DHS) Program is a key source of data on gender, women's empowerment, and reproductive health on an international scale. The DHS Program is a U.S. Agency for International Development (USAID)-funded global project that provides technical assistance to lower- and middle-income countries to collect, disseminate, analyze, and act on data related to demographics, health, and nutrition on the national and subnational levels. Launched in 1984, the DHS Program has conducted more than 400 surveys in 90 countries. Kishor said that because one of the program's key objectives is to collect high-quality data that are comparable across countries and over time, questionnaires are designed according to the guiding principle of comparability, although country-specific adjustments are also made.

DHS household surveys include five questionnaires: household, woman, man, biomarkers, and fieldworker. Kishor remarked that the DHS questionnaire for men is largely a subset of the woman's questionnaire; while both questionnaires collect information on topics including number of children, contraception, fertility preferences, and gender and women's empowerment, the woman's questionnaire includes additional questions questions related to birth (and now pregnancy) history and key indicators of maternal and child health.

Kishor presented an overview of empowerment data collected by the DHS Program since its inception. Between 1989 and 1993, the woman's questionnaire was expanded to ask gender and employment questions. Kishor herself developed the Women's Status Module, which was developed and piloted in Egypt in 1995. Around the year 2000, many empowerment variables were introduced into the core questionnaire, and optional modules on empowerment and domestic violence were developed. The number of gender-related questions in both the woman's and man's core questionnaires—as well as the number of optional modules—has continued to increase over time.

DHS questions on empowerment are designed to capture not only evidence of empowerment itself, meaning acts, attitudes, or behaviors that reveal agency, but also the contexts or settings in which women live that foster or detract from empowerment. These contextual variables include, for example, living in a household with educated members and freedom from violence, and can be used in conjunction with many indicators of evidence of empowerment itself, such as control of earnings, ownership of bank account, internet use, and control of sex.

Kishor remarked that in addition to data on empowerment, the DHS Program provides a wealth of data on other relevant topics, such as fertility and family planning. However, Kishor also recognized areas in which the DHS Program can improve its measurement and conceptualization of empowerment. A long-standing gap that DHS data does not fill is the need for longitudinal data on empowerment that can describe the causes and process of empowerment. Kishor noted that the relevance of data collected on empowerment also varies across cultures and life stages. Although the DHS Program uses country-specific indicators to account for cultural differences, the data collection needs to be more sensitive to a woman's age and marital status through the use of separate questions and methods; Kishor pointed to the fact that many DHS variables are currently applicable only to married women.

Kishor said that the DHS Program needs to collect more qualitative data to complement quantitative variables. These qualitative data will enable researchers to better decode answers related to agency, for example answers to the question, What does it mean to make a decision alone? And the question, How much value do joint actions have as evidence of empowerment? Kishor further highlighted gaps in the field's current understanding of empowerment measures, including how these empowerment measures interact with one another. Two examples of such interaction are the intersection between gender attitudes and decision-making roles, as well as between employment as empowerment and who controls earnings.

Similarly, Kishor questioned whether contraception and empowerment can be effectively studied together given the wide variation in how they relate to each other throughout the world; in some countries the use of contraception is itself a measure of empowerment, while in others it may be entirely unrelated to empowerment. Kishor suggested that this fluid relationship underlies the rarity of observing a consistently positive relationship between contraceptive use and women's empowerment across studies. Alternative "outside the box" measures of empowerment may address some of these gaps. Kishor cited leisure (or self-indulgence) as one such potential alternative measure, because it is a sign of self-worth and "true freedom." Other nontraditional indicators that may be developed to measure empowerment include hours of sleep, experience of hunger relative to men's experience, and empowerment in settings outside the household.

Kishor concluded the presentation with three key points. First, she emphasized that choice is a fundamental aspect of empowerment and challenged others to consider whether the path chosen matters for empowerment (e.g., having a sex-selective abortion, not using contraception when a child is not desired). Second, she questioned how many sets of empowerment indicators are needed to determine whether a woman is empowered, given the fact that evidence variables will differ by domain of study, location, and life stage. Finally, she posed two rhetorical questions: What does successful women's empowerment research look like? and Will we know an empowered woman when we see one—particularly in unfamiliar cultural settings? To this end, Kishor stressed the need for greater comprehension of the multidimensionality of empowerment.

During the discussion, Jocelyn Finlay asked whether researchers can propose new DHS measures to refine the work module or other survey components. Kishor said that accommodating new ideas and emerging needs is a priority for the DHS Program, and thus the questionnaires are revised approximately every five years. The program sought public feedback for the most recent revision. Although revisions are more difficult to incorporate when surveys are under way, some changes can be made at that time, particularly when a country specifically asks for an update based on its needs.

Finlay also asked whether longitudinal data can be enabled through more frequent data collection by phone or tablet. Kishor acknowledged that one lesson people are learning during the COVID-19 pandemic is how to conduct more business remotely, and that the DHS Program could look at survey approaches similar to the PMA study presented by Philip Anglewicz, in which after an in-person interview has been conducted follow-ups may be pursued by phone or with other technologies. However, Kishor said that the DHS is unlikely to ever be entirely conducted by phone because of its complexity and the sensitive nature of some of the content covered.

5

Family Planning, Fertility, and Women's Empowerment in Low- and Middle-Income Countries

Points Highlighted by the Presenters

- Investments in women's reproductive health yield large benefits for women, children, and entire societies. A methodological challenge for understanding these relationships is the endogeneity between fertility and women's employment (and between reproductive empowerment and economic empowerment). (Yana van der Meulen Rodgers, Rutgers University)
- A number of challenges are inherent to conceptualizing empowerment for research and measurement, and a limited number of qualitative studies have been undertaken to understand what empowerment means in different contexts. Studies based on large national surveys largely show mixed positive and null associations between empowerment and contraceptive use. (Yohannes Wado, African Population and Health Research Center)
- It may be time to reexamine some of the theoretical frameworks that assume that a shift from higher fertility to replacement fertility rates will result in a lasting equilibrium between fertility intentions and outcomes as well as improvements to the welfare of women and girls. The relationship between empowerment and fertility may also require closer examination. (Zeba Sathar, Population Council)
- Although low- and middle-income countries have increasingly recognized adolescent fertility as a major concern, sexual and reproductive health education is not universally available, and contraceptive use in these countries is low, despite evidence that access to contraception is key in reducing adolescent fertility. (Ndola Prata, University of California, Berkeley)

Alex Ezeh (Drexel University) served as moderator for this session, which focused on the relationships between family planning, fertility, and women's empowerment specifically in the context of low- and middle-income countries.

THE INTERSECTIONS OF WOMEN'S ECONOMIC AND REPRODUCTIVE EMPOWERMENT

Yana van der Meulen Rodgers (Rutgers University) shared that this presentation was based primarily on a recent special issue of *Feminist Economics*, for which Rodgers was a co-editor. The intersections of women's economic and reproductive empowerment were presented in a tri-level framework: *micro-level* intersections, such as decisions about contraceptive use and employment, *meso-level* intersections, such as social norms, labor marker practices, and informal sector employment, and *macro-level* intersections, such as the relationship between fertility, women's LFP, and national or regional economic growth.[1] Research in this area examines the bidirectional effect of childbearing and access to reproductive health care on women's decisions to work as well as the quality of work that is available to them and vice versa.

Rodgers outlined numerous economic benefits that result from investment in family planning or SRH. Women's access to sexual and reproductive health and rights (SRHR) often manifests in higher maternal ages at first birth, lower fertility, and longer birth spacing. This access includes but goes beyond availability of contraception, incorporating the establishment of distribution networks for contraceptives, SRH education, and family planning counseling. The effects of SRHR access are important for women's health and the economy, leading to lower costs for health systems as well as increased LFP, educational attainment, and lifetime earnings for women. Rodgers said that this research began in earnest with studies on the "power of the pill" and that similar findings have been obtained regarding the legalization of abortion.

Investment in family planning also has a positive effect on the well-being of children, Rodgers said. Lower fertility has been linked to improvements in children's nutritional status, body-mass index (BMI), developmental progress, survival rates, and educational resources. Rodgers also noted evidence that parents will invest more in their daughters when they know that their daughters will have access to contraception and abortion.

The micro-level relationship between women's economic and reproductive empowerment is described in an article from the recent special issue of *Feminist Economics* that examined the impact of quality of contraceptive

[1] S. Gammage, J. Shareen and Y. Rodgers, The intersections of women's economic and reproductive empowerment, *Feminist Economics*, 26(1), 1–22. (https://doi.org/10.1080/13545701.2019.1674451).

use on a woman's ability to work, earn money, and contribute to family income in Ethiopia.[2] Quality of contraceptive use was measured by duration and method of contraception; the authors leveraged retrospective contraceptive use history and panel data to make these determinations. The study identified a causal link between consistent contraceptive use, on the one hand, and likelihood of employment and receipt of cash payments for work (as opposed to payments-in-kind or no payment), on the other hand. Rodgers noted that this study is one of few that have paid special attention to the challenge of endogeneity, in this case by using retrospective contraceptive use history as well as panel data. A study conducted in Turkey investigated this link in the opposite direction, asking, How does employment status affect contraceptive choice?[3] That study found that employed women were more likely to use modern contraceptive methods over traditional methods, and that the effect was strongest for women who worked more secure jobs with stable incomes in the nonagricultural sector and had more access to social security and formal child care.

Rodgers shared a meso-level study that explored how the evolution of reproductive health services, social protections, and labor market institutions impact the type and quality of women's employment in 45 low- and middle-income countries.[4] The study authors identified a clear, positive relationship between unmet family planning needs and the percentage of women employed in the informal sector, as well as a similar correlation between higher rates of fertility and higher rates of informal employment. Countries that had sharp transitions in fertility did not necessarily have higher rates of women's LFP. Instead, countries that invested in health care, education, labor market institutions, and social protections produced better labor market outcomes for women. Rodgers said these findings demonstrated a critical role for coordinated policy that addresses reproductive health needs, labor market institutions, and social protections to ensure positive economic outcomes for women.

Rodgers presented another meso-level study that reached similar conclusions regarding government investments in infrastructure and women's reproductive health in India.[5] The study's mixed methods analysis of India's

---

[2] N.A. John, A.O. Tsui, and M. Roro, Quality of contraceptive use and women's paid work and earnings in peri-urban Ethiopia, *Feminist Economics* 26(1), 23–43 (doi: 10.1080/13545701.2019.1632471).

[3] D. Pekkurnaz, Employment status and contraceptive choices of women with young children in Turkey. *Feminist Economics* 26(1), 98–120. (doi: 10.1080/13545701.2019.1642505).

[4] S. Gammage, S. Joshi, and Y. van der Muelen Rodgers, The intersections of women's economic and reproductive empowerment, *Feminist Economics* 26(1), 1–22 (doi: 10.1080/13545701.2019.1674451).

[5] R.P. Pande, S. Namy, and S. Malhotra, The demographic transition and women's economic participation in Tamil Nadu, India: A Historical Case Study, *Feminist Economics* 26(1), 179–207 (doi: 10.1080/13545701.2019.1609693).

historical demographic transitions showed that declining fertility rates correlated with higher educational attainment and employment rates for women in their peak productive and reproductive years. Rodgers pointed out that even as fertility rates declined in this setting, women on average still devoted their time to motherhood; the study authors argued that a shift in focus had occurred from childbearing to *child rearing*.

At the macro level, Rodgers highlighted a study that examined fertility and LFP among immigrants and their descendants in the United States.[6] Through the use of Current Population Survey data, the study showed that the gender norms and traditions of an immigrant's home country influenced their employment and reproductive health experience in the United States, in that the fertility rate and women's LFP in the source country were associated with immigrant fertility rate and LFP in the United States. This association declined across generations, which Rodgers highlighted as evidence that gender norms are mutable and that women's LFP plays a critical role in changing these norms.

Rodgers also presented some of her own macro-level work based on DHS data from women's reproductive health diaries on abortion from 51 low- and middle-income countries.[7] Her study focused on the impact of the U.S. Global Gag Rule (renamed in 2017 as "Protecting Life in Global Health Assistance"), a policy that restricts funding for reproductive health services abroad if the recipient NGO provides abortion services, counseling, or referrals, or advocates for abortion law reform. Policies of this type have been rescinded by every Democratic president and restored by every Republican president since the Reagan administration.

Through logistic regression analysis of data collected during the George W. Bush administration, Rodgers found that countries affected by the Global Gag Rule saw increases in abortion rates—by a factor of three in Latin American and the Caribbean and a factor of two in sub-Saharan Africa—despite the stated intention of the policy to decrease abortion rates. These low- and middle-income countries have restrictive legal regimes of their own surrounding abortion, which the analysis showed was associated with higher total fertility rates, unsafe abortions, maternal mortality, and adolescent birth rates. Unsafe abortion accounts for nearly 8 percent of maternal mortality globally and as much as 10 percent in sub-Saharan Africa, Latin America, and the Caribbean. These relationships may be the result of income effects but could also be a causal result of restrictive

---

[6] F.M. Muchomba, N. Jiang, and N. Kaushal, Culture, labor supply, and fertility across immigrant generations in the United States, *Feminist Economics* 26(1), 154–178 (doi: 10.1080/13545701.2019.1633013).

[7] Y. Rodgers, *The Global Gag Rule and Women's Reproductive Health: Rhetoric versus Reality* (New York: Oxford University Press, 2018).

abortion laws. Rodgers therefore concluded that the Global Gag Rule "does not protect life at all" and that a potentially more constructive and cost-effective approach would be to integrate contraceptive care and safe abortion into the full range of reproductive health services rather than "marginalize women and their reproductive health with funding restrictions that are based purely on ideology," as she put it.

Ushma Upadhyay inquired about the effects of the U.S. Global Gag Rule in Latin America. Rodgers identified reduced access to contraception—resulting from forced closures and staff or supply shortages among clinics affected by the U.S. Global Gag Rule—as the key mediating factor that drove higher rates of both unintended pregnancies and abortions in the region.

WOMEN'S EMPOWERMENT AND FAMILY PLANNING IN SUB-SAHARAN AFRICA: REVIEW OF THE LITERATURE

Yohannes D. Wado (African Population and Health Research Center) said that an overall consensus regarding the benefits of family planning and SRH services is reflected in the United Nations Sustainable Development Goals (SDGs), which call for universal access to SRHR in accordance with the International Conference on Population and Development Programme of Action and the Beijing Platform for Action.

In sub-Saharan Africa, the use of contraception remains low, and the need for family planning and SRH services is often unmet despite recent improvements. Wado said that gender-based power imbalances are pervasive across every factor in the causal framework for unmet family planning needs, including social norms that encourage large families and early marriage, opposition to contraception by partners, low engagement of men in contraceptive efforts, and a lack of informed choice at the health services level that leads to misconceptions about contraceptive side effects.

Literature on women's empowerment and family planning in sub-Saharan Africa conceptualizes empowerment as a multidimensional and multilevel process of change that encompasses elements of agency, resources, and achievements; two commonly cited definitions of empowerment in the literature include those popularized by Naila Kabeer (London School of Economics and Political Science)[8] and the World Bank.[9] Studies generally include

[8] "The expansion of people's ability to make strategic life choices in a context where this ability was previously denied to them" (N. Kabeer, Resources, agency, and achievements: Reflections on the measurement of women's empowerment, *Development and Change 30*(3), 435–464.)

[9] "The process of enhancing individuals or group's capacity to make purposive choices and to transform those choices into desired actions and outcomes" (R. Alsop and N. Heinsohn, *Measuring Empowerment in Practice: Structuring Analysis and Framing Indicators* [World Bank, 2005] [doi: 10.1596/1813-9450-3510]).

one or more dimensions of empowerment: economic (e.g., women's control over income, access to and control of family resources); sociocultural (e.g., freedom of movement, lack of discrimination against daughters); familial or interpersonal (e.g., participation in domestic decision-making, control over sexual relations, freedom from domestic violence); legal (e.g., knowledge of rights, domestic support for exercising rights); political (e.g., political awareness, access, voting rights); or psychological (e.g., self-esteem, self-efficacy, well-being).

Wado examined the correlation between a country's aggregate-level gender inequality index and contraceptive prevalence. The index captures reproductive health, empowerment, and status, with a higher index indicating greater disparity between males and females. Many countries in sub-Saharan Africa have a high gender inequality index (>0.5) that correlates with low contraceptive use. Only Rwanda, Namibia, and South Africa have gender inequality indices below 0.5, and all three countries have higher rates of contraceptive use. Wado noted that some countries where contraceptive use is high, including Zimbabwe, still have high gender inequality indices. In an analysis of DHS indicators of women's empowerment and reproductive health outcomes, a moderate correlation was observed between contraceptive use and the percentage of married women who participate in household decision making.

Wado presented findings from several studies that show differing degrees of relationship between women's empowerment and contraceptive use. A meta-analysis that collected DHS data on women's empowerment and contraceptive use in 33 developing countries, 19 of which are in sub-Saharan Africa,[10] revealed a positive and significant relationship between women's decision-making autonomy and contraceptive use. It found that women with higher empowerment scores were more likely to use modern contraception in 8 of these 19 sub-Saharan African countries. Another study that leveraged DHS data from five African countries generated empowerment scores based on six dimensions of empowerment indicators and found a strong association between overall empowerment scores and contraceptive use; however, Wado noted that only countries with high contraceptive prevalence were included in that study.[11] In a third study that aggregated DHS data from 34 sub-Saharan African countries, three dimensions of women's empowerment (attitude toward violence, social independence, and decision making) were developed using principal component

[10] S. Ahmed, A.A. Creanga, D.G. Gillespie, and A.O. Tsui, Economic status, education and empowerment: implications for maternal health service utilization in developing countries, *PLOS ONE 5*(6), e11190 (doi: 10.1371/journal.pone.0011190).

[11] M. Do and N. Kurimoto, Women's empowerment and choice of contraceptive methods in selected African countries, *International Perspectives on Sexual and Reproductive Health 38*(1), 23–33 (doi: 10.1363/3802312; PMID: 22481146).

analysis based on 15 items from the DHS Empowerment Module and other status indicators.[12] The analysis showed that attitudes toward violence and decision making were more consistently associated with modern contraceptive use than social independence. In the fourth and final study that Wado cited, pooled DHS data based on multi-level empowerment indicators from 32 sub-Saharan African countries indicated that decision-making autonomy and LFP were positively associated with contraceptive use in all examined countries, and that the rates of contraceptive use were higher in countries with a moderate score on the human development index.

Wado explained that data on covert use of contraception are also of interest to empowerment research because they have implications for decision-making autonomy. Studies dating to the 1990s show that covert use of contraceptives is a common practice. A recent study currently under review leveraged two rounds of PMA data collected in Kenya and showed that 12.2 percent of women were engaging in covert use of contraception.[13] This practice was more common among older women (ages 35–49) and in individuals of low socioeconomic status. Injectables and implants were among the most common contraceptive methods used covertly, and these methods are also the ones driving the rise in contraceptive use in sub-Saharan Africa.

Wado concluded his presentation by underscoring the challenges inherent in conceptualizing empowerment for research and measurement, pointing to a limited set of qualitative studies that describe what empowerment means in different contexts and noting that the common method of aggregating or pooling data from different countries may mask contextual variations. Wado echoed the call for programming that engages both men and women in efforts to expand contraceptive use in sub-Saharan Africa.

In the discussion, Nancy Birdsall commented that there is no question about the high association between empowerment and contraceptive use, as well as between education and formal employment and contraceptive use, in sub-Saharan Africa. Birdsall then asked whether the ultimate cause of these relationships is known. Wado noted that his review focused on empowerment and family planning outcomes, but acknowledged that education and employment are key variables. Rates of education and modern-sector employment in sub-Saharan Africa are low, although Wado pointed out that relationships between contraceptive use and employment are more inconsistent than associations with educational attainment, possibly because

[12] F. Ewerling, J.W. Lynch, C.G. Victora, A. van Eerdewijk, M. Tyszler, and A.J.D. Barros, The SWPER index for women's empowerment in Africa: development and validation of an index based on survey data, *Lancet Global Health* 5(2017), e916–e923.

[13] C. Akoth, J.O. Oguta, and S.M. Gatimu, (under review), Prevalence and determinants of covert contraceptive use in Kenya: A cross-sectional study.

conceptualizations of "employment" (e.g., formal vs. informal) may distort the observable relationship between employment and contraceptive use in the region. Wado said that the causes of low education and employment levels are complex and related to the level of development in sub-Saharan Africa as well as political commitments to education, women's employment, and family planning. In francophone Africa in particular, wars and conflicts in the region further weaken this political commitment.

FAMILY PLANNING, FERTILITY, AND WOMEN'S EMPOWERMENT

Zeba A. Sathar (Population Council) said that it is time to challenge some of the theoretical frameworks, such as the Demographic Transition Theory, that assume that a shift from higher fertility to replacement-level fertility rates will result in a lasting equilibrium between fertility intentions and outcomes as well as improvements to the welfare of women and girls. The "demographic dividend"—the economic growth potential that can result from shifts in a population's age structure[14]—is often cited as one explanation for how fertility decline can have a beneficial impact on women, children, and household welfare: in this model, that decline promotes women's LFP and household savings. However, Sathar posited that fertility decline does not predict other aspects of women's welfare. For example, sex-selective abortion and gender violence continue even in contexts of low fertility.

In addition, Sathar said, the relationship between empowerment and fertility may require closer examination. Individual-level measurements of women's empowerment and autonomy have operated relatively well for decades, and women's empowerment does correlate strongly with contraception and fertility (with positive and negative correlations, respectively). However, Sathar noted, the factors that influence the outliers in these data are unclear. Why do some countries, such as Nepal and Bangladesh, demonstrate higher levels of contraceptive use and lower fertility rates than their levels of women's empowerment would predict, while other countries, such as Afghanistan and Pakistan, show the opposite deviation from the model?

Several other correlations between contraceptive use and specific empowerment measures may be useful in further analyzing this relationship. For example, contraceptive use correlates strongly with female adult literacy rates and freedom from physical or sexual violence. In addition, a strong direct correlation exists between the total fertility rate and gender violence, including physical and sexual violence. A weaker correlation exists between contraceptive use and women's LFP—perhaps due to variation in types of employment.

[14] United Nations Population Fund. http://unfpa.org/demographic-dividend.

Sathar more specifically examined anomalous data regarding family planning in Asia, a region that shows wide variation in family planning effort (FPE) indices across countries. Proper measurement of these efforts would require incorporation of more gender-related indicators into data collection and analysis. Nonetheless, the classic correlation patterns exist between contraceptive use or total fertility rate and the FPE index (i.e., FPE is highly correlated with contraceptive use and inversely correlated with total fertility rate, although the latter correlation is weaker). However, marriage patterns in Asian countries represent an anomaly. Although countries with higher rates of contraceptive use and lower total fertility rates may be expected to also have higher ages at first marriage, this expectation is not always born out.

In Bangladesh, more than half of women are married by age 18 despite high contraceptive use and low fertility, while in Pakistan, a country with relatively low rates of contraceptive use and high fertility, only 18 percent of women are married by the same age. Similarly, other indicators of women's empowerment, such as domestic violence rates, fail to follow expected correlations with total fertility rates and contraceptive use. Sathar emphasized that the field needs to understand the regional drivers of marriage patterns and commonly used empowerment measures through more nuanced and qualitative studies to understand what these sorts of indicators mean for women's empowerment and autonomy.

Sathar suggested that theoretical frameworks evolve toward a multidimensional perspective, one that encompasses changes in fertility and contraceptive use alongside variation in women's and girls' autonomy or welfare. Furthermore, she cautioned against placing greater value on reaching a demographic state-of-replacement fertility than on reaching an ideal equilibrium of women's and girls' welfare as it relates to fertility intentions and outcomes. Some aspects of family planning programs can be modified now based on existing data, such as the power relationships between women and providers as well as the incorporation of domestic violence prevention. Finally, Sathar asked workshop attendees to agree on a minimum number of agency measures that are necessary to achieve autonomy and resist family and societal pressure toward negative outcomes, such as unwanted sex, pregnancy, marriage, or violence.

In the discussion, Ann Blanc (Steering Committee Chair, Population Council) asked Sathar to elaborate on how the burdens of caring for children and the elderly mediate the relationship between LFP and childbearing. Sathar referenced a study conducted in India in which women's LFP declined in spite of lower fertility rates, and identified child care as a mediating factor in this complicated relationship. She noted that childcare duties, as well as care for older parents, often fall to women and subsequently decrease women's LFP.

FERTILITY, FAMILY PLANNING, AND EMPOWERMENT: THE CASE OF ADOLESCENTS

Ndola Prata (University of California, Berkeley) described adolescence as an important time during which people experiment with independence, forge new relationships, develop new social skills, and learn new behaviors. It is therefore important to engage adolescents in meaningful ways—including through support for SRH—that may encourage healthy transitions to adulthood.

According to the United Nations, adolescent birth rates have declined since 1990, although variation throughout the world is considerable and rates remain high in many low- and middle-income countries. The decline in adolescent birth rate has also been slower than the decline in the total fertility rate in some areas. Prata underlined that although early marriage is a strong underlying factor, not all childbearing among married adolescents is intended and sexual initiation before marriage is almost universal. High levels of adolescent fertility are associated with a high proportion of unsatisfied demand for family planning, and longer duration of schooling—particularly for girls—has been linked to lower levels of adolescent fertility.

The United Nations Population Division has reported that the governments of low- and middle-income countries have increasingly recognized adolescent fertility as a major concern.[15] However, comprehensive SRH education is not universally available and contraceptive use in low- and middle-income countries is low, despite evidence that access to contraception is a key element in reducing adolescent fertility. A recent review estimated that approximately 23 million girls (ages 15–19) in low- and middle-income countries have an unmet need for contraception.[16] Prata said that meeting this need would decrease the number of unwanted pregnancies and unsafe abortions as well as improve overall reproductive health outcomes.

Prata presented an analytic framework to study adolescent reproductive health that identifies the key drivers of adolescent fertility as unsafe sexual practices, specifically lack of contraception, and harmful practices, such as child marriage and female genital mutilation. The framework also outlines the underlying causes or social determinants that contribute to these drivers to highlight potentially effective areas of programmatic intervention. These underlying causes include poverty, attitudes that prevent safe sexual practices, lack of education, health system bottlenecks, and gender discrimination. Prata noted that these drivers may not contribute equally in all regions to reproductive outcomes, such as unsafe abortion and sexually

---

[15] United Nations Department of Economic and Social Affairs, Population Division, *World Population Policies* (2013).

[16] J. Deitch and L. Stark, Adolescent demand for contraception and family planning services in low- and middle-income countries: a systematic review, *Global Public Health 14*(9), 1316–1334 (doi: 10.1080/17441692.2019.1583264; Epub 2019 Feb 22; PMID: 30794484).

transmitted infections (STIs), or to individual, household, or community-level consequences, such as maternal morbidity and mortality, adolescent offspring mortality, and increasing poverty. For example, harmful practices are less common in Angola than in Niger, but both countries have high fertility driven by a lack of contraceptive use.

Prata introduced a second framework to conceptualize the adolescent contraceptive journey. This framework recognizes documented differences in contraceptive access and utilization among adolescents depending on whether they are unmarried, married without children, or married with children. The framework is designed to identify opportunities at the micro, meso, and macro levels across these three important subgroups. For example, the norms of a community may dictate very different contraceptive access for an adolescent who is unmarried than for one who is married (e.g., based on norms surrounding sexual activity), or even for two married adolescents when one does and the other does not already have children (e.g., access to contraception once desired family size has been met).

Different approaches employed to improve adolescent empowerment have focused on areas such as asset building, attitudes and capabilities, conditions and opportunities, and economic assistance. Prata focused on youth participation in SRH policies and programs, citing the United Nations' recognition of adolescent participation in matters that concern them directly or indirectly as a fundamental right. Four essential and interconnected features of meaningful adolescent participation have been outlined by the United Nations: *space* (i.e., safe and inclusive opportunity to form and express views), *voice* (i.e., expression of views facilitated freely in a medium of choice), *audience* (i.e., listening to adolescent views), and *influence* (i.e., appropriate action based on adolescent views). Prata highlighted three categories of participation as it relates to empowerment: empowerment *within* (e.g., self-efficacy, dignity, recognition of entitlement), empowerment *with* (e.g., building partnerships, solidarity), and empowerment *to* (e.g., challenging violations, influencing decisions, realizing rights, and holding duty bearers accountable). Prata emphasized that the empowerment *to* category of participation is especially important for adolescent SRH.

Outcomes for meaningful participation can be aggregated into three groups: consultative, collaborative, and adolescent-led. Prata said that ideally the voice and agency features of adolescent participation in SRH matters would be adolescent-led, but noted work by the United Nations Children's Fund (UNICEF) to develop consultative and collaborative strategies for adolescents of both genders to participate in the prevention of child marriage.

Increased availability of contraception to adolescents represents an economic opportunity for low- and middle-income countries. Improved contraceptive access empowers healthier and more educated young adults and decreases fertility, alleviating rapid population growth and poverty. Furthermore, this access allows low- and middle-income countries to harness the demographic dividend. Prata said a great deal of evidence supports interventions that will help low- and middle-income countries to reduce adolescent fertility, including longer duration of education, comprehensive sex education, universal health care for adolescent SRH (including wide contraceptive access), adolescent empowerment, abolition of harmful practices, and promotion of gender equity.

In the discussion, Caroline Kabiru (African Population and Health Research Center) asked how SRH services and rights differ for adolescent girls and young women, including by marital status, commenting that the association between early marriage and contraceptive use in Bangladesh, for example, may not be surprising because it is perhaps more acceptable for a married (rather than unmarried) adolescent girl to use contraception. Prata confirmed that married adolescents, regardless of age, in sub-Saharan Africa and South Asia have relatively better access to SRH service than unmarried adolescents. However, adolescent girls are pressured to have multiple children after marriage. Education on the importance of birth spacing to the health of mothers and children has increased use of contraception by young married mothers, but Prata said that in countries with high fertility rates and low contraceptive prevalence, such as Angola and Niger, young women will sometimes have four or five children before seeking family planning counsel.

6

Mechanisms of Attitude Change

Points Highlighted by the Presenters

- Results from an intervention program in Bangladesh focused on empowering early-adolescent girls (through education support, gender awareness, and livelihood skills) suggest that the program increased empowerment among girls and served as an equalizer, in terms of wealth and other differences, across girls. (Sajeda Amin, Population Council)
- It may be necessary for family planning interventions to operate within existing gender norms; there is scope for change even without progress on gender norms. (Sarah Baird, George Washington University)
- Social norms research and norms-based interventions should consider what social norms-based intervention to improve modern contraceptive use looks like; how interventions to be run in communities with low collective norms should be differentiated from those in communities with high collective norms; and how the power of interpersonal communication can be harnessed to amplify normative influences. (Rajiv Rimal, Johns Hopkins University)

Jocelyn Finlay (Harvard University) served as moderator for this session. She explained that presenters would focus on the following question: What are the mechanisms by which changes in attitudes toward and opportunities for girls and women affect changes in attitudes toward and use of contraceptives (and vice versa)?

SKILLS THAT EMPOWER: MEASURING ATTITUDINAL CHANGE IN THE CONTEXT OF INTERVENTIONS IN BANGLADESH

While empowerment is an important goal for adolescent girls' programming, empowerment remains elusive and unobserved in most quantitative surveys. Sajeda Amin (Population Council) presented results from a study that measured patterns of empowerment among early adolescent girls in Bangladesh, which ranks fourth-highest in the world and the highest in Asia in rates of child marriage. The study was based on data from the Bangladeshi Association for Lifeskill Income and Knowledge for Adolescents (BALIKA) Program. BALIKA aims to impart skills and build empowerment for girls with the goal of changing child marriage.

However, many of the empowerment indicators used in this analysis were based on research on *women's* empowerment, so an important goal of the analysis was to determine whether these same constructs could also be adapted to adolescent girls. Specifically, the analysis focused on three central questions:

1. Do distinct classes of empowerment emerge among girls in early adolescence, and if so, how are they characterized?
2. Are background characteristics of wealth, parental education, religion, and marital status predictive of latent class membership?
3. Did the BALIKA project's different skill-building strategies influence girls' probability of belonging to a certain class of empowerment?

BALIKA is an intervention-based research project that tested three intervention strategies—education support, gender awareness, and livelihood skills—in a cluster-randomized controlled trial within 96 Bangladeshi villages. BALIKA leveraged considerable community engagement in all intervention arms, though the skills emphasized were different. Qualitative and quantitative data were collected from 9,000 girls (ages 12–19) from 2013 to 2015 (with a 14.1% attrition from baseline to endline). Amin said that BALIKA had a striking impact on child marriage, with a 30 percent reduction in all intervention arms compared to controls.

Outcome measures from BALIKA included workforce participation, time spent in school, learning outcomes (numeracy and English), school retention, child marriage, and empowerment. Amin highlighted that the gender awareness intervention arm appeared to have the most consistently positive impact on these outcome measures compared to the other two interventions, particularly on time spent in school, workforce participation, and learning outcomes.

To assess empowerment, the project used multiple indicators of mobility (e.g., access to school, adolescent center or NGO, library, playground), social support (e.g., networks of friends), participation in society (e.g., affiliation with community groups or sports), freedom from family domination (e.g., ability to socialize with people from other religions, ability to disagree with parents), and access to information (e.g., recent TV watching, mobile phone ownership, basic computer skills). Two attitudinal measures—attitude toward gender roles and attitude toward violence—were also included. Latent class analysis was used to identify relationships between these seven classes of empowerment indicators. A latent class regression analysis was used to assess predictors of class membership and included four background characteristics for each girl: household wealth, marital status, religion, and parents' level of education. The BALIKA study arm (i.e., gender, education, livelihood, control) was also considered.

The analysis revealed three distinct classes of girls at baseline. One class (about one-third) provided relatively unempowered responses to the survey. The second class of girls was very mobile and socially active but also very accepting of traditional gender roles and violence. The third class of girls—while less mobile and social than the second class—had more progressive attitudes toward gender roles and violence. At endline, a fourth class of girls emerged; nearly one-third of the girls shifted toward more empowered responses on both the mobility and social indicators as well as the attitudinal indicators. Household wealth was associated with class membership at baseline but not at endline, whereas marital status, religious affiliation, and parents' education level were predictive of class membership throughout; more empowered girls tended to be unmarried and non-Muslim and to have parents with more education. The BALIKA study arm was also predictive of class membership; girls who participated in the gender awareness and education support arms were significantly more likely to belong to the emergent fourth, most empowered class.

Overall, BALIKA increased empowerment among girls: the proportion of girls belonging to the least empowered class diminished from 32 percent to 17 percent after the BALIKA intervention. Furthermore, Amin described BALIKA as an equalizer that promoted empowerment, in terms of both wealth and other differences, across girls.

EXPERIMENTAL EVIDENCE ON CHANGING GENDER NORMS, TACKLING MISINFORMATION, AND DECREASING COSTS: IMPLICATIONS FOR FAMILY PLANNING

Sarah Baird (George Washington University) enumerated several demand-side drivers of family planning for women in low- and middle-income countries, including opportunities in employment and education, misinformation (e.g., inadequate family planning counseling, provider bias, misunderstanding of risks), poverty, and gender and social norms. These drivers interact in important and complicated ways that necessitate multi-pronged, context-dependent approaches to identify solutions, which Baird pointed out may require long-term research given that drivers such as gender norms are slow to change. Baird shared the following definition of gender norms from a recent paper, noting that some interventions will try to improve family planning outcomes by operating within gender norms while others will attempt to change them:

> Gender norms are social norms defining acceptable and appropriate actions for women and men in a given group or society. They are embedded in formal and informal institutions, nested in the mind, and produced and reproduced through social interaction. They play a role in shaping women's and men's often unequal access to resources and freedoms, thus affecting their voice, power, and sense of self.[1]

Baird presented evidence from several studies of family planning intervention efforts. The first was a 2014 experiment that provided married women in Zambia with vouchers for free contraception.[2] The intervention attempted to work within existing gender norms by varying whether women were given access to contraceptives alone or with their husbands. Couple treatment resulted in less uptake of family planning services and higher fertility than individual treatment, but Baird noted that these improved family planning outcomes in the individual treatment arm came at a cost of lower reported subjective well-being. This implies a psychosocial cost of concealing contraceptive treatment. In a second study, adolescent development clubs in Uganda provided girls with vocational training and information on sex, reproduction, and marriage.[3] Researchers surveyed and tracked a representative sample of around 5,000 adolescents. The intervention appeared to delay marriage and childbearing at a four-year follow-up, but it did not increase contraceptive use among sexually active girls. It is also important to note that, despite low levels of empowerment at baseline, only 21 percent of girls signed onto the program, and attrition was high at 35 percent. A third study gave non-financial incentives to hair dressers to increase sales of female condoms in Zambia; condom sales were rewarded with stars that indicate contribution to the health of the

---

[1] B. Cislaghi and L. Heise, Using social norms theory for health promotion in low-income countries, *Health Promotion International 34*, 616–623.

[2] N. Ashraf, E. Field, and J. Lee, Household bargaining and excess fertility: an experimental study in Zambia, *American Economic Review 104*(7), 2210–2237.

[3] O. Bandiera, N. Buehren, R. Burgess, et al., Women's empowerment in action: evidence from a randomized control trial in Africa, *American Economic Journal: Applied Economics 12*(1), 210–259.

community.[4] Baird appreciated that this approach utilized small nudges within existing structures to promote improved family planning outcomes.

Baird also highlighted four ongoing studies that are in preliminary stages. The first study is a collaboration with BRAC in Tanzania to examine three interventions targeting contraceptive uptake and SRH outcomes for unmarried adolescents: providing free contraceptives to females, empowering females through a goal-setting exercise related to staying healthy and HIV/STI-free, and engaging with boyfriends, through soccer, to educate them about healthy intimate relationships.[5] So far, the study authors have found that engaging males and goal-setting exercises has improved intimate-partner violence outcomes but has not affected uptake of contraceptives or fertility outcomes. Baird remarked that even though this supply-side intervention provides contraceptives free of charge, it has had no impact on pregnancy-related outcomes, likely because of a very low contraceptive prevalence at baseline (<1%), which did not substantially change at endline. Baird offered lack of engagement with mothers—who were generally not happy about the free contraception intervention—as a potential explanation for this result, as well as misinformation about contraceptive side effects.

A second ongoing study seeks to increase the uptake of long-acting reversible contraceptives (LARCs) among adolescents and young women in Cameroon.[6] This pilot qualitative study is highlighting the attitudes of providers, mothers, and young women that create barriers to LARC uptake—namely, that family planning is not relevant for young, unmarried women without children. Misinformation about side effects and price of contraception in Cameroon were also identified as barriers. In response, the study is pursuing two interventions: first, a shift in family planning counseling strategy from an informed-choice model (i.e., clients are given information about all options and given a choice) to a shared decision-making model (i.e., clients relate their family planning goals and medical histories to the provider and then receive a recommendation); and second, price discounts for the LARCs. Quantitative pilot information has revealed that adolescents and adults who are already seeking family planning will pursue LARCs at any of the offered price points. When clients already had

---

[4] N. Ashraf, O. Bandiera, and B.K. Jack, No margin, no mission? A field experiment on incentives for public service delivery, *Journal of Public Economics 120*, 1–17.

[5] M. Shah and J. Seager, Promoting safe sex among adolescents in Tanzania (AEA RCT Registry, September 23, 2020 (doi: 10.1257/rct.1305-6.1999999999999999).

[6] B. Özler, S. Athey, and J. Jamison, Increasing the uptake of long-acting reversible contraceptives (LARCs) among adolescent females and young women in Cameroon. Ongoing; Also see: B. Özler, An adaptive experiment to improve quality in contraceptive counseling and increase the uptake of long-acting reversible contraceptive methods, Seminar Presentation, Available: https://www.worldbank.org/en/programs/sief-trust-fund/brief/seminars#07212020.

a contraceptive type in mind, they were more likely to take up a LARC when it was free or discounted than at its regular price. When clients did not have a specific contraceptive in mind, tailored counseling increased uptake of LARCs, but only at higher price points (at lower prices there was no evidence of increased uptake). Adolescents and adults who arrive at a health facility for non-family-planning reasons are considerably more likely to take up LARCs at lower prices. A large-scale randomized controlled trial is scheduled to occur in 2021.

Baird is personally working on the third ongoing study she presented, which targets first-time young mothers as a possible entry point for increased family planning uptake in Bangladesh and Tanzania. Baird said that this intervention strategy recognizes that the norms preventing adolescents from engaging with family planning before their first birth may be too difficult to change, and instead focuses on postpartum family planning. She said that she and her colleagues are developing program enhancements on the demand and supply sides that will work within existing platforms. Barrier and facilitator analyses have revealed similar barriers as found in other studies, including social and gender norms, harsh and judgmental attitudes, myths about family planning, and missed opportunities to integrate postpartum family planning.

Baird is also working on a fourth ongoing study in Ethiopia, which aims to conduct interventions among very young adolescents who tackle gender norms alongside their peers, families, communities, and broader institutional structures. The two-year multilevel program, known as Act With Her Ethiopia (AWH-E), will include curriculum-based programming and will operate according to the Gender and Adolescence: Global Evidence (GAGE) framework.[7] Baird explained that the study will be a cluster-randomized trial in which intervention arms are defined by increasing levels of engagement: first for girls only, then with the addition of boys and parents, then the addition of community and systems strengthening, and finally with the addition of asset transfers. Preliminary findings have shown strong short-term impacts on voice and agency, knowledge, and nutrition, but less evidence of changing gender attitudes and norms. Baird noted that the adolescents in this study are particularly young and may not be sexually active or menstruating, but that funding will allow the study to track the influence of early intervention as the adolescents enter those life stages.

In the discussion, Ann Blanc (Steering Committee Chair, Population Council) asked how long the AWH-E Program will follow the girls and whether the timeline will encompass multiple "transitions" to adulthood, such as leaving school, marriage, and first birth. Baird replied that the project has funding through 2024 (for a total of nine years), at which point

[7] See https://www.gage.odi.org.

the girls will be ages 17–19. The project could be funded for an additional five years, at which point the girls will be ages 22–24.

Jocelyn Finlay inquired about the role of stigma in accessing family planning interventions. Baird responded that the BRAC collaboration in Tanzania addressed stigma in the goal-setting and male engagement intervention arms. She noted that the LARC study in Cameroon may already be working with a more empowered group of women because they have already visited the health facility in the first place. Stigma will be addressed once the supply-side intervention is working robustly and the focus shifts slightly toward bringing in women who have not yet visited the health facility.

SOCIAL NORMS AS DRIVERS OF MODERN CONTRACEPTIVE USE: WHAT WE KNOW AND HOW WE USE THIS INFORMATION

Rajiv N. Rimal (Johns Hopkins University) defined three varieties of social norms: *descriptive norms* (beliefs about what most others do), *injunctive norms* (pressures to conform), and *collective norms* (what others actually do). Rimal commented that more research currently exists on descriptive and injunctive norms—which are alike in that they are both based on perceptions—than on collective norms.

Research on social norms investigates the normative influence that these norms—whether perceived or objective—have on behavior. The power of normative influence varies based on individual-level factors (e.g., self-efficacy, perceived benefits), behavioral attributes (e.g., public vs. private behaviors, addictiveness of behaviors), and contextual characteristics (e.g., time constraints, external monitoring). Consequently, norms are more important in some contexts than others and to some people more than to others. Rimal explained that these elements are captured by the Theory of Normative Social Behavior, in which these three classes of moderating factors are unpacked in an effort to understand the conditions in which social norms are more or less influential than others.[8]

Social norms also interact to modulate their relative influence. Injunctive norms, for example, may amplify the effects of descriptive norms. Rimal illustrated this dynamic in a scenario of college drinking behavior: students are more likely to consume alcohol when they believe that many others drink (i.e., high descriptive norm) and that there is pressure on themselves to conform (i.e., strong injunctive norm); when the pressures are not

---

[8] R.N. Rimal and K. Real, How behaviors are influenced by perceived norms: a test of the Theory of Normative Social Behavior, *Communication Research* 32(3), 389–414 (https://doi.org/10.1177/0093650205275385); A. Chung, and R.N. Rimal, Social norms: A review, *Review of Communication Research* 4, 1–29.

felt, the influence of believing that everyone else drinks is less powerful.[9] Similar patterns exist with regard to perceived benefits of a behavior. For example, college students who perceive a large benefit to consuming alcohol, such as a social benefit of conforming, are more likely to be influenced by the perception that many others drink, while those who do not perceive a benefit in the activity are not especially subjected to this normative influence.[10] In this case, perceived benefits have both a main effect and interaction with descriptive norms.

Rimal considered this framework in relation to research on normative influence on contraceptive use. A recent study in Ethiopia demonstrated the reliable association of both descriptive and injunctive norms with condom use by young men.[11] Another study in India examined interpersonal communication—and in particular spousal communication—as a potential amplifier of normative influence on the choices of women.[12] In this latter study, spousal communication heightened the influence of descriptive norms among women with one child. Similarly, this interpersonal communication amplified the influence of injunctive norms for all categories of women studied: women with zero, one, or two or more children.

Research on collective norms is relatively new. Rimal highlighted a study conducted in Germany in 2019 that examined the role of all three classes of norms on the texting and driving behaviors of adolescents.[13] This study revealed that descriptive norms are more consequential among adolescents whose social groups objectively engage in more risky behavior, whereas descriptive norms have little effect in social networks that do not engage in these behaviors. Similar effects have been seen in the realm of modern contraceptive use. An analysis of DHS data from Ethiopia and Tanzania demonstrated that women who live in communities with high rates of contraceptive use are also more likely to use modern contraception themselves.[14]

---

[9] R.N. Rimal and K. Real, Understanding the influence of perceived norms on behaviors, *Communication Theory 13*(2) (https://doi.org/10.1111/j.1486-2885.2003.tb00288.x).

[10] R.N. Rimal, Modeling the relationship between descriptive norms and behaviors: a test and extension of the theory of Normative Social Behavior (TNSB), *Health Communication 23*(2), 103–116 (doi: 10.1080/10410230801967791).

[11] A. Jain, H. Ismail, E. Tobey, and A. Erulkar, Stigma as a barrier to family planning use among married youth in Ethiopia, *Journal of Biosocial Science 51*(4), 505–519.

[12] R.N. Rimal, P. Sripad, I.S. Speizer, and L.M. Calhoun, Interpersonal communication as an agent of normative influence: a mixed method study among the urban poor in India, *Reproductive Health, 12*, 71 (doi: 10.1186/s12978-015-0061-4).

[13] S. Geber, E. Baumann, F. Czerwinski, and C. Klimmt, The effects of social norms among peer groups on risk behavior: a multilevel approach to differentiate perceived and collective norms, *Communication Research* (doi: 10.1177/0093650218824213).

[14] E. Sedlander and R.N. Rimal, Beyond individual-level theorizing in social norms research: how collective norms and media access affect adolescents' use of contraception, *Journal of Adolescent Health 64*(4), S31–S36.

Rimal explained that this relationship between the collective norm and individual behavior was stronger in more isolated communities, suggesting that individuals with less access to the outside world are more likely to follow community norms.

Rimal illustrated the various ways in which perceptions interact with reality in the context of modern contraceptive use, as well as potential opportunities for intervention in each case. Women who believe that most other women do not use contraception when in fact most others do are demonstrating pluralistic ignorance rather than accurate perception. In situations of pluralistic ignorance, Rimal said that descriptive norm-based interventions (in which people's misperceptions are corrected) should be enacted. When women accurately perceive that most other women do not use contraception, interventions should highlight the aspirational few who do. On the other hand, women who believe that most other women use contraception when in fact most others do not are experiencing the false consensus effect as opposed to accurate perception. In these cases, interventions should address barriers to use of modern contraception, and reinforced social support should be provided for women whose perception of reality is accurate.

Rimal ended the presentation with three questions that should be considered when conducting social norms research and designing norms-based interventions: First, what do social norms–based interventions to improve modern contraceptive use look like? Second, how can these interventions be differentiated between communities with low and those with high collective norms? And third, How can the power of interpersonal communication be harnessed to amplify normative influences?

In the discussion, Megan O'Donnell (Center for Global Development) asked how media, such as radio and TV shows, could serve as a way to reach more isolated communities to increase exposure to more gender-equal norms. Rimal cited a study of isolated communities in Nepal that demonstrated that collective norms are strongly correlated with people's perceptions of those norms.[15] Access to media likely serves as a role model for different manners of behavior that may not have been in the cognitive repertoire of women in these communities. Given the enormous importance of norms in isolated communities for providing information, social influence, and social sanction, Rimal pointed out that media can also empower women by providing examples of how to handle normative backlash.

Nancy Birdsall noted a study of Saudi husbands who are themselves comfortable with their wives working but believe that most other husbands

[15] R.N. Rimal, A. Chung, and N. Dhungana, Media as educator, media as disruptor: conceptualizing the role of social context in media effects, *Journal of Communication 65*, 863–887 (doi:10.1111/jcom.12175).

oppose wives in the workforce. Rimal cited a similar finding of pluralistic ignorance from the late 1960s, in which White American families reported that they were comfortable with their children playing with the children of a neighboring Black family, but that they did not believe their other neighbors would feel the same way.[16] In these situations, correcting the misperception can to some extent change the behaviors.

[16] Angus Campbell, *White Attitudes toward Black People*, Ann Arbor, Michigan, Institute for Social Research, 1971, pp. 135-136.

7

Foundation and Agency Programs and Priorities

Sunita Kishor (ICF) served as moderator for this session, which focused on the work and priorities of agencies and foundations that fund work in this area.

WILLIAM AND FLORA HEWLETT FOUNDATION

Althea Anderson serves as a Program Officer for the William and Flora Hewlett Foundation's Global Development and Population Program, where she manages research and advocacy grant making for international reproductive health and women's economic empowerment. Anderson also represented the Foundation at the Workshop on Reproductive Health and Global Development in May 2020. Anderson shared several links to resources describing the foundation's evolving grant-making strategies.[1]

The Hewlett Foundation refreshes its grant-making strategies approximately every five years. Refreshes are designed to evaluate current strategies, characterize progress, assess the evolution of the field over the previous five years, and shape the strategy for the next 5 years to create possible synergies across the Global Development and Population Program. An evaluation and refresh of the foundation's international reproductive health (IRH) and women's economic empowerment strategies was launched in March 2020. The evaluation found that the Hewlett Foundation's reputation and contribution to sexual reproductive health and rights (SRHR) progress has been largely defined by its sub-strategies in francophone west Africa

[1] See Hewlett Foundation at http://hewlett.org.

and its approach to local advocacy field-building in west and east Africa. Grantees agree that the Hewlett Foundation has made a marked difference in francophone west Africa by contributing to doubling voluntary contraceptive use in the nine Ouagadougou Partnership countries. Anderson said that Hewlett has also enabled several service delivery and advocacy organizations to expand operations in this sub-region. The Hewlett Foundation has seeded experimental approaches to improving service delivery and encouraging peer donors to scale these programs. For example, it has done work in human-centered design with IDEO.org and Marie Stopes International, which has expanded from Zambia to Kenya, the Sahel, and beyond.

Progress has been observed in Hewlett Foundation research initiatives that engage potential evidence users, leading to the eventual application of evidence for policy change and practice. The most promising cases engaged evidence users early in research design processes and aimed for applied and user-focused research with strong links to advocacy initiatives. Anderson highlighted the opportunity to further explore the role of research in supporting advocacy and service delivery.

The evaluation also found that the Hewlett Foundation is perceived by some stakeholders as more grounded in a women's rights and reproductive rights framework compared to other reproductive health and family planning donors. Anderson hypothesized that this centralization of women's aspirations and their relationships to reproductive health (as compared to a purely demographic approach to reproductive health) may be important for changing gender and social norms to support sustained changes in reproductive health outcomes.

Anderson shared findings from the Hewlett Foundation's global and Africa regional landscape scans. SRHR remains critical for women, their families, and their communities because it supports and is associated with women's and girls' agency, health, educational attainment, and economic opportunity. The past decade has seen significant growth and use of SRHR services due to sustained focus and investments. Anderson said that continued support will expand current innovations—including community-based delivery, self-managed care, integration with other services, improvements to quality of care by addressing provider bias, and technology-enabled service delivery (e.g., telemedicine)—to further expand SRHR. New product innovation largely focuses on contraception, although Anderson noted that medication abortion is a major innovation that has expanded access to safe abortion around the world.

Anderson highlighted growing support to align reproductive health momentum with governments' desire to capture a demographic dividend but reported that progress has been slow. Nonetheless, maintaining continued progress on SRHR may necessitate a strong enabling environment. Anderson explained the value of addressing demand-side factors, such as knowledge and awareness building, while simultaneously shaping partner dynamics, engaging cultural influencers, and shifting gender and social norms.

Despite this progress, Anderson said, global opposition to reproductive health is rising and expanding from an anti-abortion focus to a broader opposition to gender equity and rights. All stakeholders acknowledged that more needs to be done to mitigate this opposition, including strengthening regional and in-country SRHR research and advocacy to address sensitive issues with government and other decision makers with greater credibility. The Maputo Protocol and other African regional commitments increasingly support gender equity and SRHR, and Anderson said this presents an opportunity for governments to push for related policies and investment.

Anderson suggested that research could focus on uptake of findings to inform advocacy, policy, and programming. She noted that the most effective research is often conducted in close partnership with ministries of health and finance, technical working groups, and key stakeholders, so that research is designed to address evidence users' questions and is primed to shift policies and practices. This approach typically benefits from strong regional and in-country research capacity through sustainable institutions. Anderson also identified a gap in user research dedicated to better understanding what kinds of contraceptive access women want as well as what women's broad aspirations and life goals are.

The Hewlett Foundation has reviewed these findings over the weeks leading up to the workshop and is beginning the next phase of the IRH strategy refresh. Anderson shared some areas of inquiry for future grant-making and framing. First, the foundation is considering broadening its strategic goal to deliberately position reproductive health within the broader context of women's lives, well-being, and aspirations. To that end, Anderson asked workshop participants how the foundation should think about positioning its work in this broader context, and inquired how other donors have adopted a rights-based women's empowerment grant-making approach and balanced it with the more traditional framing around family planning that remains prevalent globally. The second area of inquiry is increasing reproductive health demand. The Hewlett Foundation IRH strategy will continue to focus on expanding access to contraception and safe abortion, but also seeks to contribute to demand generation by considering the foundation's role in reaching new contraceptive users. Anderson said that the Hewlett Foundation can play a leading role in expanding access to safe abortion with the introduction of medication abortion and is investigating ways to capitalize on this opportunity.

The Hewlett Foundation also wants to strengthen the enabling environment for SRHR. Anderson recognized that multiple influencers, including intimate partners, families, communities, and societies, can support girls' and women's agency and well-being, including access to reproductive health care. Thus, the Hewlett Foundation is exploring ways to leverage its investments for impact at these various scales in order to contribute to an enabling environment in which women can achieve their aspirations through reproductive agency. In addition, the foundation strives to continue to bridge the gap between knowledge production and evidence use and seeks opportunities at regional and national levels. New investments will aim to ensure that evidence users are integrated throughout the research process to meaningfully inform policy and practice.

Anderson said that the Hewlett Foundation is exploring synergies between the IRH and women's economic empowerment strategies to expand current investments, including linkages between women's reproductive choices and their economic agency. In the women's economic empowerment strategy refresh, the Hewlett Foundation will explore new investments to ensure the availability of accurate data and a sound empirical base of evidence on women's unpaid work to inform more gender-aware macroeconomic and social benefit policies. The foundation has learned that researchers have struggled to meaningfully engage advocates, practitioners, and policymakers to value and use evidence on women's unpaid work. Integrative analyses on women's unpaid work and reproductive choices are limited, so this intersection is not often considered in national policies.

The Hewlett Foundation is also exploring its role in reimagining global development. Anderson said that the field, including SRHR, is undergoing a necessary period of reckoning with a focus on shifts of power, influence, and decision-making from global to national to regional actors. The foundation is considering its role in this process given its niche and values and will finalize and disseminate its new strategy in the second and third quarters of 2021.

In the discussion, Megan O'Donnell expressed an interest in strengthening linkages between evidence generation and use through communication between researchers and evidence users, and she asked how the Hewlett Foundation and other donors may encourage that communication. Anderson responded that the Hewlett Foundation has required nearly all of its grantee partners for IRH and women's economic empowerment research investments to include a robust research uptake plan that clearly outlines which evidence users will be engaged and how they will be engaged throughout the research process. The foundation also asks researchers which regional and national policymakers, decision-makers, and advocates have shown a demonstrated interest in that evidence. Tamara Kreinin added that the Packard Foundation partners global researchers with local researchers, in part to provide mentorship to local researchers with less of a global presence and also to bring global researchers closer to evidence users and policymakers; in that way, she said, Packard Foundation funding is "practical research for advocacy."

Nancy Birdsall asked how U.S.-based donors are reacting to the risk of a continuing decline of reproductive rights in the United States. Anderson responded that USAID's global development team—and particularly the women's choices pillar—has done some scenario planning to determine what the possible impacts of the 2020 election may mean for USAID investments. Anderson noted that some policy advocacy investments have shifted to work on changing cultural narratives in the United States, specifically in the American South.

UNITED NATIONS POPULATION FUND

Benoit Kalasa presented an overview of five programming priorities for the United Nations Population Fund (UNFPA). UNFPA's strategic plan is framed within a Decade of Action that sets a 10-year horizon for achieving its SDGs by 2030. When UNFPA adopted the SDGs, it urged the world to consider the life of a 10-year-old girl and what she would need to fulfill her potential. This motivational framework is intended to prompt nations to consider the health and well-being of young girls as their national economies grow. The principle of leaving no one behind and reaching those furthest behind first permeates the strategic plan. To uphold this principle, UNFPA believes that it must meet the needs of the estimated 270 million women who want to avoid pregnancy but are not using safe and effective family planning methods. Kalasa said that UNFPA has focused on three transformative goals: ending the unmet need for family planning, ending preventable maternal mortality, and ending harmful practices, such as gender-based violence. Kalasa noted that UNFPA is also interested in observing the intersection among these three goals.

UNFPA's SDG Target 5.6 is to ensure universal access to SRHR. This target includes two indicators. Target 5.6.1 centers on the proportion of women ages 15-49 who make their own informed decisions regarding sexual relations, contraceptive use, and reproductive health care. Target 5.6.2 focuses on the number of countries with laws and regulations that guarantee full and equal access of women and men ages 15 and older to SRH care, information, and education. Kalasa said that research on both of these indicators has revealed major challenges and helped UNFPA identify where greater effort is needed. For example, 97 out of 107 countries surveyed have laws and regulations that guarantee access to contraceptive services; however, 28 percent of these countries have minimum age requirements to access contraceptive services, and 21 percent have restrictions based on third-party authorization. Data monitoring is key to inform future work to advance the rights and choices of women.

UNFPA is also working in the area of demographic dividends. This effort seeks to ensure that young people realize their rights to decide whether and when to have children and to achieve the related promise of economic growth. The Sahel Women's Empowerment and Demographic Dividend (SWEDD) collaborative program with the World Bank was implemented in six countries in west Africa to examine how adolescent girls' and adult women's economic autonomy and education enable them to access information and services related to SRHR. The program is expanding into another 3 countries, and through the Human Capital Plan will eventually reach up to 25 countries. Kalasa said this expansion was important to determine how countries can leverage their domestic resources to support SRHR and that the UNFPA is building more partnerships and synergies.

Through the UNFPA Supplies Program, contraceptives are procured and distributed to 46 priority countries. This program benefits from many donors and key partnerships, including the Bill & Melinda Gates Foundation. Kalasa said that UNFPA is working on a new vision for this program, which will assess the learnings from the past decade in order to meet the goal of ending unmet family planning needs and preventable maternal mortality by increasing equitable access to high-quality modern contraceptives and life-saving maternal health. The SRHR of women are at the center of this program, which is built around a compact of accountability and leadership across government, civil society, the private sector, and the United Nations.

Rebuilding after the COVID-19 pandemic is the final program priority Kalasa presented. At UNFPA, the response to COVID-19 has focused on preserving momentum on three strategic priorities: supporting continuity of SRH services, addressing gender-based violence, and maintaining the supply of modern contraceptives and reproductive health commodities. Kalasa said that UNFPA is working with governments and key partners on a concerted effort to mitigate the impact of the pandemic by ensuring that SRHR services are considered essential services during COVID-19 response—for example, through availability of personal protective equipment (PPE) for health and family planning providers, supply-chain preservation for reproductive health products, and continuation of rights-based family planning services that offer a range of contraceptive services.

As UNFPA enters the Decade of Action to achieve the SDGs, it is fully committed to continuing to support countries and uphold the rights of individuals—especially women—to plan their families. UNFPA is striving to end all unmet need for voluntary family planning by 2030, and Kalasa reiterated the need for continued collaboration and research to achieve this goal.

Sunita Kishor asked how UNFPA can ensure that governments do indeed work within the women's rights framework. Kalasa replied that human rights are a basic principle for United Nations work and that UNFPA representatives' core focus is to monitor and advance SRHR. UNFPA also seeks to engage women and youth organizations in that advocacy.

DAVID AND LUCILE PACKARD FOUNDATION

Tamara Kreinin said that the David and Lucile Packard Foundation works on a continuum of reproductive health rights and justice. The Packard family and foundation team articulate a set of core values that drive their approach to these issues, including investment in strong leadership, integrity, and a sense of equity and justice. The foundation's programs focus heavily on context, with all funded locations having local advisors and, in the case of Addis Ababa, a full office. These local advisors inform the foundation of national and regional needs and changes. They also perform "beyond the check" work, holding conferences and meeting with governments, funders, and civil societies within the local context, which elevates the foundation's initiatives. Efforts are evidence-based and increasingly performed through a justice and equity lens.

The Packard Foundation has operated within the framework of a consistent strategy for the past eight years and will present a new strategy in 2022. Partners and experts in the field will help to evaluate the foundation's work and provide context, information, and evidence to inform the new strategy. A new president was instated on August 31, 2020, and Kreinin noted a generational shift on the board. During the past six months, following the COVID-19 pandemic and murders of Black men and women in the United States, the Packard Foundation board has called for an even more focused evaluation of how the foundation's work interacts with this justice lens.

The Packard Foundation tends to fund services, policy, advocacy, organizing, shifting of social norms and communication, and research. The Foundation operates in sub-Saharan Africa (Ethiopia, Rwanda, Kinshasa DRC), south Asia (India, Myanmar), and the United States (primarily Louisiana and Mississippi). Kreinin noted that work in all regions is mutually informative. The foundation's work includes a range of SRHR and justice initiatives. This range begins with sexuality education through a gendered lens and a trauma-informed emphasis on resilience. This approach is based on research that indicates the inclusion of gender, trauma, and resilience in sexuality education increases its impact. Kreinin highlighted the goal of providing youth-friendly services and ending child marriage with this generation. Contraception and family planning are also part of the foundation's work, and Kreinin recognized the need for a focus on both concepts separately, given that most young people do not want to plan a family but do want contraception. The Packard Foundation considers abortion to be a part of contraceptive services in an ideal world.

The Packard Foundation's work is aligned according to two primary threads. The first thread of work is related to quality, which Kreinin said is centered on rights and includes good counseling, the ability to switch contraceptive methods without question, a lack of provider bias, and contraceptive availability and choice. The Foundation is following a patient-centered approach, which Kreinin noted is meant to be adapted to the specific geography of the recipient population. Kreinin acknowledged that women who do not experience quality are more likely to walk away from SRH services and health care services in general. The Packard Foundation also considers quality as it relates to stigma. Kreinin pointed out that although the foundation's focus on stigma began with abortion-related stigma, it has now expanded to stigma related to all contraception, family planning, and sexuality education. The second thread of the foundation's work focuses on young people, both as recipients of services and information and as leaders, activists, and movement builders.

Kreinin said that cross-issue mobilizing is increasingly the goal of young people and that the Packard Foundation is working to understand the impacts of that form of mobilization on reproductive health services and policies. Kreinin also commented on ongoing efforts to research and facilitate culture and norm shifts, for example by using the arts to stimulate conversations about abortion in Louisiana.

The Packard Foundation is cognizant of opposition to its efforts, which Kreinin recognized has surged recently around the globe. The foundation is also focused on humanitarian settings that are homes for internally displaced individuals and refugees. Kreinin said the foundation is working to increase sexuality education, delay early marriage, and ensure that women have access to contraceptive services and abortion in those contexts.

Universal access to health care is a priority for the Packard Foundation, with an emphasis on SRHR. This priority has expanded to encompass research on access to and quality of telemedicine, particularly in light of the COVID-19 pandemic. Kreinin acknowledged that marginalized women often do not have access to the technology or privacy needed to take advantage of telemedicine. The Packard Foundation has commissioned research on telemedicine in India to better understand meaningful delivery of telemedicine to vulnerable populations. The foundation is also committed to self-care and self-administered or over-the-counter contraceptive services, including medication abortions and contraceptives through delivery mechanisms such as Sayana Press. Kreinin recognized the potential for governments to claim that women do not need facilities or counseling because of the availability of self-administered solutions, and noted that the foundation seeks to provide women with choices and an ability to obtain information for themselves.

Kreinin concluded by reiterating that the Packard Foundation increasingly focuses on justice and equity, particularly as they intersect with funded outcomes related to family planning, abortion, and sexuality education.

In the discussion, Ann Blanc asked whether the Packard Foundation has considered how to practically aim for improvements in both reproductive health outcomes and justice and equity, for example by determining important indicators of justice and equity. Kreinin responded that the foundation is shifting funding to address this issue: first, through a focus on ensuring that the most vulnerable and marginalized individuals receive high-quality services and care, and second, through power-building movements that elevate the voices of those individuals. For example, when the foundation discovered that some of its work in India was not reaching the poorest communities, it intentionally shifted its work to reach those communities and further adapted the work to maintain quality in the new context. The Packard Foundation also funds reproductive justice groups in the American South and aims to add funding that will support dual outcomes related to equity and justice as well as reproductive health. Kreinin emphasized the importance of intersectional movement-building, predicated on the notion that (to paraphrase Audre Lorde) women do not lead single-issue lives.

Nancy Birdsall asked how U.S.-based donors are reacting to the risk of a continuing decline of reproductive rights in the United States. Kreinin said that the Packard Foundation has long funded both global and U.S. work and that the board increased U.S. funding efforts after the most recent change in administration. The foundation has also started a collaborative on gender and reproductive equity based on the premise that American SRHR advocates are undersupported, underfunded, and overwhelmed. To that end, the Packard Foundation has committed an extra $50 million over five years and has engaged other foundations as well as individual philanthropists to bring more funds into the field. In addition, the foundation has an increased interest in the American South, where the region's health disparities (particularly in Louisiana) intersect with the gender, equity, and justice lens that the foundation is increasingly using to guide its efforts. Kreinin added that the foundation's global work is instructive for the U.S. context.

OFFICE OF POPULATION AND REPRODUCTIVE HEALTH, USAID

Afeefa Abdur-Rahman is an institutional contractor who serves as a senior gender advisor in the Office of Population and Reproductive Health (PRH) in the Global Health Bureau at USAID. USAID maintains that investing in women's economic empowerment builds countries that are resilient and self-reliant, because an investment in a woman is an investment in her community and her country. The Women's Economic Empowerment Act of 2018 requires gender analyses to shape USAID strategies and projects in all sectors. USAID's family planning programs support the right of individuals and couples to make and act on decisions about whether and when to have children. Thus, the principles of voluntarism and informed choice are central to the USAID vision and mission. Abdur-Rahman said that USAID investments strengthen countries' capacities to provide family planning information, services, and modern methods as well as create enabling environments, including more gender-equitable norms that will allow people to achieve their reproductive intentions. Abdur-Rahman pointed out that abortion is not a part of USAID family planning programming.

Abdur-Rahman said that voluntary family planning programs that expand choice, promote dialogue, and empower clients to make decisions that meet their individual needs contribute to their overall empowerment. Abdur-Rahman further recognized that expanding women's access to contraception improves women's health and creates opportunities beyond childbearing, including the ability to access education and participate fully in the workforce. Family planning also helps women time and space pregnancies to ensure healthy outcomes for themselves and their children. At the societal and national levels, voluntary family planning contributes to economic growth and population resource balance.

To make and act on voluntary, informed family planning decisions, Abdur-Rahman said individuals must have access to accurate family planning information, be able to choose whether to use contraceptives, and have access to a range of contraceptive methods and services. The goal of PRH's empowerment work is to engage with individuals, families, communities, and health systems to improve both gender equality outcomes and to help women, men, and couples achieve their reproductive intentions. Abdur-Rahman said that an empowered individual or couple that voluntarily uses contraception that matches their current intentions at that particular time is at the center of that goal.

Given the role of gender norms, power dynamics, and inequalities in how individuals navigate reproduction and contraception use, PRH has prioritized three technical areas to improve gender dynamics across the life course and enhance family planning outcomes: reproductive empowerment (i.e., informed choice, voice, and power to act on fertility desires without fear of violence), male engagement (i.e., men as users, supportive partners, and agents of change in a way that centralizes gender and power dynamics), and gender-based violence (GBV) mitigation (i.e., prevention of and response to GBV in the family planning context).

Abdur-Rahman explained that PRH interventions within these three priorities promote and increase women's empowerment in myriad ways that overlap with and reinforce each other. Interventions address women's power *within* (e.g., women's knowledge of family planning; self-awareness and self-worth; expectation of a supportive partner, healthy relationships, and quality health care), power *to* (e.g., ability to voice intentions to partners and agency to engage in decision-making and strengthened supportive environments where male partners are empowered to nurture women's agency), and power *with* (e.g., collective action to achieve fertility desires and advocacy for improved access to family planning care). Abdur-Rahman highlighted another dimension—power *over* (i.e., addressing threats to women's agency)—as a cross-cutting element under PRH's three gender priorities.

Outcomes of PRH's family planning and empowerment work will manifest at multiple levels. At the individual level, outcomes include but are not limited to access to resources, agency, attitudes toward family planning and family planning methods, self-efficacy, body literacy, and fertility behavior. At the relationship level, outcomes can address couple dynamics and relationship quality, communication, and decision making. At the community level, programs can measure shifts in gender norms and changes in collective actions to hold leaders and health systems accountable. At the systems level, interventions are geared toward outcomes related to provider competency to offer respectful, non-judgmental, and gender-sensitive services; gender norms; gender-transformative support supervision; and reduction of discrimination and harassment in the workforce. At the policy level, work can measure the extent to which health policies and budgets are gender-responsive with the goal of empowerment of women, men, and couples.

Abdur-Rahman highlighted several illustrative approaches that PRH has supported that contribute to empowerment, engage men, and mitigate gender-based violence. One such intervention in Kenya, Addressing Reproductive Coercion in Health Settings (ARCHES), was a pilot clinic-based model that enabled providers to identify reproductive coercion and intimate partner violence among women seeking family planning counseling, as well as provide targeted voluntary family planning counseling and referrals for follow-up support. A second intervention supported the development and testing of two digital health tools: Smart Couple and Smart Client. These tools used prerecorded interactive voice response calls, SMS, and entertainment education to provide women and men with education that prepares them to access voluntary family planning services and encourages conversation about family planning. In Uganda, a third initiative supported the Gender Roles, Equality and Transformation (GREAT) Project, a community-based intervention that addressed the link between unequal gender norms and reproductive health in married and unmarried youth. The GREAT Project improved gender-equitable attitudes, family planning use, and male engagement in child care and household chores. In east Africa, a fourth effort has supported methodologies that strengthen leadership, advocacy, and accountability skills of women leaders and helped those women to foster joint accountability for family planning within health systems. In a fifth example, PRH invested in developing a framework and training modality that offers a set of competencies for providers to offer gender-equitable service provision that empowers clients.

PRH aims to harmonize its empowerment principles with new voluntary family planning service delivery efforts that intersect with other health areas, including maternal and child health, nutrition, and health care, including in fragile settings. Moving forward, PRH will also continue to support development of measures of agency and empowerment and will use those measures in more projects and countries to refine measurement and understand how interventions influence agency and decision-making. Based on existing evidence and theory, PRH is also supporting the development of a theory of change for male engagement in family planning, including pathways to gender equality, agency, and empowerment and family planning outcomes for both women and men. Sunita Kishor added that USAID also funds the Demographic Health Surveys.

In the discussion, Megan O'Donnell expressed concern with the way that family planning is positioned within the USAID draft gender policy in its reference to family planning only in the context of marriage. Abdur-Rahman responded that interest in this updated policy has been tremendous and that USAID appreciates the attention and interest in ensuring the policy is as strong as possible. She added that USAID was in the process of reviewing comments on the updated policy (at the time of the workshop). The review process is being directed by Julie Cram (Senior Coordinator for Gender Equality and Women's Empowerment) and Sarah Gesiriech (Special Advisor on Children in Adversity).

BILL & MELINDA GATES FOUNDATION

Ann Starrs shared that the family planning strategy at the Bill & Melinda Gates Foundation has undergone a year-long refresh that is slated for completion by early 2021. The Gates Foundation is committed to maintaining a funding level of $280 million per year for family planning. One significant change to the budget is a ramping up of investment in contraceptive technology research and development, which will comprise 30 percent of the budget moving forward.

The Gates Foundation family planning strategy is anchored in understanding women's and young people's preferences and priorities, which is critical to addressing their reproductive needs. Starrs clarified that although the Gates Foundation uses the term *family planning*, its strategy focuses on access to and use of contraception. The strategy is based on three broad elements of the Gates Foundation's theory of change. The first element is the expansion of contraceptive method choice, which is the basis for the budget increase to promote contraceptive technology research and development. Starrs recognized that women's concerns about contraceptive side effects are a major barrier to use and continued use of contraception. Technology is a key part of the foundation's overall comparative advantage and focus, and the goal of this research and development effort is to adapt existing and develop new contraceptive methods that will eliminate or reduce the side-effects barrier. Expansion of contraceptive method choices requires access to the range of contraceptive methods, and to that end the Gates Foundation will also study issues related to market shaping, launching, and the availability of new products and to supply chain issues as well to ensure access for women and young people.

The second element is to optimize family planning interventions on both the supply and demand side to address barriers that prevent women and young people from making and acting on decisions for their reproductive intentions. This effort revolves around providing knowledge about contraceptive methods and building supportive family, community, and broader contexts to facilitate decision-making. The Gates Foundation is also investigating the role of the private sector in expanding and maximizing access to appropriate contraception and is exploring the expansion of access to self-care methods, driven in part by the recent COVID-19 pandemic.

The third element of the theory of change maximizes access to high-impact interventions through and with scaling levels. This expansion of access involves work with a range of partners in the global family planning ecosystem to promote the adoption and scaling of high-impact family planning practices, both established and novel. These three strategic elements of the theory of change are supported by cross-cutting work on data and accountability as well as advocacy.

Starrs reported that the Gates Foundation brought its family planning, maternal/newborn child health, and nutrition teams into a cluster in 2019 (currently called FP/MNCH/nutrition). The three teams retain their independent budgets, workstreams, and strategies, but the clustering is intended to highlight opportunities for linkages and streamlining, such as in postpartum family planning. In January 2020, the Gates Foundation also established a new division on gender equality; its inaugural president, whose tenure will begin in November 2020, will develop the focus for that division. Starrs recognized the clear bidirectional linkages between the goals of the family planning strategy and gender equality. In addition, the foundation is having an ongoing conversation surrounding diversity, equity, and inclusion related to its own structures, policies, and internal culture, as well as implications for partnership and voice.

Starrs acknowledged that the Gates Foundation has a significant budget and said that its resources will be applied to what the foundation considers to be its comparative advantage and value-add. The key elements and priorities of the family planning strategy are shaped by this rationale. Starrs emphasized that elements left out of the strategy for this reason are neither inherently viewed as unimportant by the Gates Foundation nor will they be entirely excluded from the conceptual framework of the strategy.

Starrs also noted that historically, much of the Gates Foundation's work has been driven out of Seattle. Moving forward, although Seattle will remain a central location, country-specific strategies in focus geographies—especially those that have a country office—will be more clearly anchored in those countries.

8

Key Themes and Next Steps

Ann Blanc (Steering Committee Chair, Population Council) introduced the final session, during which the steering committee members reflected upon the highlights and key themes of the workshop. Opportunities that emerged from the workshop for potential future work in this area were also discussed.

Amy Tsui, Johns Hopkins University (emerita)

Tsui commented on the sense of urgency regarding the application of empowerment constructs in the field and juxtaposed that urgency with the fact that the research and science will take time to demonstrate their effects. Tsui said that this workshop presents a unique opportunity to advance conceptualizations of women's empowerment, consider outliers (as in the presentation by Zeba Sathar), test measurement approaches, and assess different hypotheses about the impact of women's empowerment as a process. Although rigorous projects that have already generated evidence were shared at the workshop, the evidence remains episodic. A systematic way of testing women's empowerment could help convince governments and other sponsors that this area deserves investment.

Tsui reiterated that women's empowerment is a multidimensional process that manifests at different levels of society and across cultural contexts. She outlined three specific gap areas in which research could be conducted. First, research could examine how contraceptive use relates to women's LFP in terms of quality, duration, and earnings potential. This examination would require longitudinal data that captures work, fertility, and contraceptive events over the life course to bypass the potential role of endogeneity (i.e., in cross-sectional research). Second, research could form a knowledge base that encompasses the breadth of the women's empowerment construct and the multiple actors involved in women's social and reproductive choices over the course of a lifetime. Tsui emphasized that women's empowerment is not a one-method intervention, such as contraception, nor simply a policy, such as universal schooling or safe motherhood policies, but is rather a human development process. Third, research may systematically include men and young boys in the process of empowering women's choices, decisions, and achievements. The influence of these male roles should be based on empirical evidence. Tsui concluded by applauding the strength of female leadership in this field, which was demonstrated during this workshop.

Sunita Kishor, ICF

Kishor reinforced the importance of the context in which women and men live and interact to ensuring the welfare of individual women and girls. The focus on women's empowerment is rightly placed, but women do not exist in isolation. The importance of context leads to questions about what it really means to make a decision "alone" and about the frequent focus on whether a woman is partnered or unpartnered. Kishor also acknowledged that the field tends to be somewhat prescriptive when discussing SRHR and women's empowerment. Kishor mentioned the presentation by Anita Raj and said that it is important to determine what women's needs actually are instead of being prescriptive about those needs; for example, SRHR addresses not only using contraception but also infertility. Empowerment comes in the form of a woman being able to fulfill her own fertility desires and having the access and resources to do so. The focus on unmet need—which Kishor recognized as a research construct that does not necessarily explain why women do not use contraception—must be approached carefully and holistically.

Kishor emphasized the importance of institutions and norms even when examining data collected at the individual level. Many women have to act as pioneers in order to change discriminatory norms, often for the sake of their daughters—these pioneering women need institutions that actually build on and enable these norm changes. After all, the ability to get an education for your child and have children enjoy their childhood should not be revolutionary and if institutions were supportive, women would not have to be pioneers and face many challenges to meet these goals. Kishor also expressed concern about the difficulty of distinguishing outcome variables from empowerment indicators. This difficulty is another articulation of the endogeneity issue and challenges the field to reflect on how it defines empowerment.

Kishor concluded by acknowledging that many conceptualizations of women's empowerment depend on research in Asia, and that as a result many traditional indicators of empowerment or disempowerment may not apply in other contexts. For example, measures of mobility may be less relevant in African contexts than in Asian contexts. These cross-cultural differences are an ongoing challenge in this field of study.

Jocelyn Finlay, Harvard University

Reflecting on Tsui's call for male inclusion in women's empowerment research, Finlay noted that women are nested within couples and/or communities and must often negotiate with men. Therefore, inclusion of men in empowerment research and interventions is an inherent aspect of carefully considering a woman's context. She added that it is also important to recognize that men want to be a part of the process of empowering women.

Finlay commented that this workshop demonstrated recent successes and opportunities in this field. In particular, Finlay highlighted advances in the measurement of empowerment. However, the data currently utilized by many researchers could be reinvigorated by technological advances that render paper surveys outdated. New technologies could enable swifter data collection and longitudinal assessments. Finlay argued that more frequent measurements from smaller studies also offer some advantages compared to broader cross-sectional data collection and may allow researchers to study questions related to mechanisms of empowerment rather than merely its prevalence.

Finlay cited a question from Zeba Sathar regarding the relative adequacy of theoretical frameworks. Finlay's own work began with research on the demographic dividend, which was discussed at multiple points throughout the workshop. Finlay reasoned that a strong, mathematically based theoretical foundation supports the ongoing push to conduct rights-based research; this foundation will ensure that researchers speak the same language and perform work that can be empirically validated.

Finlay cautioned that researchers must be aware of unintended consequences of interventions when the mechanisms for success are not fully understood. Differences in sample size, context, or timing, for example, can distort an intervention's expected effect.

Alex Ezeh, Drexel University

Ezeh underscored the importance of generating data and developing measurements of empowerment constructs. In addition, he echoed the calls of his colleagues for more longitudinal data to assess the relationships explored in this workshop, that is, across women's SRHR, LFP, and empowerment. He also emphasized the importance of measurements at the society level. While women's empowerment is measured largely at the individual level, he said, this workshop has demonstrated the many external factors, such as social norms, that influence these individual measures.

Ezeh suggested that researchers consider the impact of the COVID-19 pandemic on both demographic research and data collection efforts. Much of this work relies on face-to-face interviews and may need to be rearranged in the future to avoid disruptions to data collection. On a related topic, leveraging natural experiments would depend on more careful study design. For example, in some regions very similar populations live in neighboring countries yet experience very different outcomes (e.g., Burundi and Rwanda, Equatorial Guinea and Gabon). This pattern creates an opportunity to conduct national-level research to identify factors that influence divergent outcomes in otherwise similar countries.

One driver of high fertility in African contexts, Ezeh said, is the relatively young age at first marriage and first birth. Although interventional programs exist for adolescents who are in school or are married, he questioned how to reach unmarried adolescents who do not attend school, who represent a large proportion of adolescents in countries such as Niger and Chad. Interventions are particularly effective at transitional stages, such as the progression from primary to secondary school, and Ezeh highlighted the opportunity to understand the circumstances of adolescents who do not make this progression and to assess their relative access to these interventional programs.

Ezeh prioritized a shift from global to local priorities. The DHS Program has existed for nearly 40 years, yet he challenged whether many countries have the institutional capacity to drive change based on the findings of its surveys. Additional support for local institutions would help them drive the ongoing conversation surrounding SRHR and empowerment. Ezeh also pointed out two contrasting demographic patterns that are currently occurring: many high-income countries face large reductions in population over the next few decades, while other countries continue to demonstrate high fertility and rates of population growth. The implications of this change are not well understood, and coping with these trends requires a global perspective, investment, and response.

Mayra Buvinic, United Nations Foundation

Buvinic expressed admiration for the quality of the research progress, especially on determinants and measurements, presented at this workshop. Buvinic also outlined a number of challenges facing future research. First, the measurement of women's economic empowerment at the group and collective levels, compared to the individual level, remains a challenge. Various domains of empowerment could also be more explicitly recognized and delineated to clarify whether a study centers on overall empowerment, economic empowerment, social empowerment, or another domain altogether. These domains may require different forms of measurement and have varying degrees of overlap. Buvinic recognized that measures may need to be adapted or created to capture the processes of disempowerment provoked by the COVID-19 pandemic. Buvinic added that the Center for Global Development and Data2X recently drafted a compendium of empirically derived women's empowerment–related measures with more than 34 associated methodologies and tools. The volume of data, methodologies, and tools identified and aggregated in the compendium suggests a potential for harmonization within the research community to establish common practices and shared measures. Buvinic stressed the importance of an open data approach to this effort.

Second, insufficient research exists to answer the question of how reproductive health choice relates to empowerment. Buvinic said that although increasingly good evidence is available on this subject, it remains unclear whether agency in reproductive health choices generalizes to economic empowerment and vice versa.

Third, research could grapple more fully with the instrumental aspect of empowerment. Across the realms of reproductive autonomy, economic agency, or other domains entirely, small changes in empowerment can have large instrumental impacts on women's lives. Buvinic suggested that researchers continue to work toward identifying the triggers for this instrumental aspect of empowerment. Buvinic also supported longitudinal studies of empowerment, particularly to determine the sustainability of empowerment over time, as well as how to make empowerment more sustainable than it currently appears to be.

Buvinic concluded with a call for research on how behavior influences social norms, acknowledging that much work already exists examining the reverse relationship, that is, how social norms influence behavior. Behavior is the trigger for changes in social norms, and thus studies can help to identify the behavioral attributes that drive social transformation.

Nancy Birdsall, Center for Global Development

Birdsall recalled the 1986 NASEM report that Win Brown referenced during the opening of the workshop and observed that a complete reframing of family planning and women's relationship to it has occurred since that report was published. To encapsulate the current framing, Birdsall posed the following syllogism:

A. Female autonomy and empowerment are key to a better world for everybody.

B. Reproductive rights are key to female autonomy, because women do not have the same access to sexual intercourse without fear of pregnancy as men and because early pregnancy has long-term implications for women's empowerment and rights.
C. Thus, access to reproductive rights, contraception, and justice in these domains is key to a better world.

In keeping with this reasoning, Birdsall emphasized a rights-based conceptual approach to research on reproductive rights and women's empowerment.

Birdsall suggested that some confusion persists about the relationship between agency and empowerment. To Birdsall, agency is one key dimension of empowerment, but empowerment requires more than agency, as well; for example, it also requires control and resources. Both agency and empowerment could be better measured at the collective and political level. Research at this level also raises the question of the relative importance of social attitudes and norms versus economic development in different societies. While structural aspects of a community, such as economics and education, change slowly, social norms can change quickly. More research would help identify the triggers and mechanisms that underlie these changes and their relationships to each other.

Finally, Birdsall acknowledged that conducting more longitudinal work is not an easy feat, but she suggested a possible role in this effort for the Committee on Population. In the short term, the calendar work from DHS may shed light on questions of empowerment over the life course of women. She also called for more exploitation of natural experiments, citing COVID-19 and the #MeToo movement as recent global starting points for such work.

Ann Blanc, Steering Committee Chair, Population Council

Blanc concluded the workshop by recognizing progress in both the sophistication and nuance in conceptual work on women's empowerment. To put this work to use, Blanc called for more studies on the pathways that link women's empowerment to SRH outcomes and posed several questions to guide future research directions:

- What are the roles of changing attitudes and gender norms on the pathway to better SRH outcomes?
- What is the mediating effect of caring for children and the elderly on women's LFP and on empowerment more broadly?
- What is the potential for working with boys and men to change gender norms?

- What are the ways that the linkages between women's empowerment and SRH outcomes vary systematically across contexts, and how can that variation be explained?

Blanc commented on the influence of the COVID-19 pandemic on gender equality by sharing an anecdote in which a talented prospective hire recently turned down a job at the Population Council out of concern that the current circumstances (i.e., the pandemic) would diminish her capability to perform her duties; the anecdote, like the pandemic itself, throws the unequal responsibility of caring for children and the elderly into sharp relief. Blanc also noted that the gender-specific implications of climate change were not discussed at this workshop, although they are linked to reproductive health outcomes. This nascent area deserves attention from researchers and donors.

Blanc also joined the chorus of support for longitudinal studies of women's empowerment. Blanc remarked that she worked on a 1985 report on women's employment and fertility that outlined the limitations of cross-sectional data, highlighting a long-standing opportunity for donors to support longitudinal work. Although cross-sectional surveys such as those performed by the DHS are valuable and fulfill their intended functions, they will not help overcome the endogeneity problem that obscures causal relationships in the empowerment process. More investment in randomized experimental studies is important, and longer-term studies may also be needed to determine the sustainability of empowerment and whether completed interventions have lasting effects.

Appendix

Agenda

Workshop on Family Planning, Women's Empowerment, and Population and Societal Impacts

September 24–25, 2020

THURSDAY, SEPTEMBER 24

10:00–10:10 am EDT

Welcome and goals for the workshop
Malay Majmundar, Director, Committee on Population
Ann Blanc, Steering Committee Chair, Population Council

10:10–10:20 am EDT

Background on the workshop
Win Brown, Bill & Melinda Gates Foundation

10:20–11:30 am EDT

The role of fertility decline and women's empowerment in economic development and in other population and societal changes
Moderator: Amy Tsui, Johns Hopkins University (emerita)

This session will focus on questions such as:

- What is the link between fertility change and economic development, especially at the macro level?

- What is the role of women's empowerment as an intervening variable?
- What do we know about the relationship between changes in the role of and status of women in developing countries, and economic growth?
- Has access to family planning mattered?

Jocelyn Finlay, Harvard University
Naila Kabeer, London School of Economics
Seema Jayachandran, Northwestern University

11:30–11:45 am EDT
Break

11:45 am–1:15 pm EDT
Measuring women's empowerment
Moderator: Mayra Buvinic, United Nations Foundation

This session will focus on questions such as:

- What are the ways in which women's empowerment is measured and operationalized?
    - At what level is empowerment measured?
    - Proxies for measuring women's agency

Ushma Upadhyay, University of California, San Francisco
Sonalde Desai, University of Maryland
Kathryn Yount, Emory University
Aletheia Donald, Africa Gender Innovation Lab, World Bank

1:15–2:10 pm EDT
Break

2:10–3:20 pm EDT
Ways of addressing current data limitations
Moderator: Nancy Birdsall, Center for Global Development

This session will focus on questions such as:

- What are the key data sources for studying the relationship between contraceptive use, fertility, and women's empowerment?
- What are the key data limitations, and how might they be addressed?

Philip Anglewicz, Johns Hopkins University
Anita Raj, University of California, San Diego
Sunita Kishor, ICF

3:20–3:30 pm EDT

Wrap-up day 1 and plans for day 2
Ann Blanc, Steering Committee Chair, Population Council

FRIDAY, SEPTEMBER 25

10:00–11:20 am EDT

Family planning, fertility, and women's empowerment in low- and middle-income countries
Moderator: Alex Ezeh, Drexel University

This session will focus on the extent to which the nexus between family planning, fertility, and women's empowerment varies within and across low- and middle-income countries.

Yana van der Meulen Rodgers, Rutgers University
Yohannes Wado, African Population and Health Research Center, Nairobi, Kenya
Zeba Sathar, Population Council, Islamabad, Pakistan
Ndola Prata, University of California, Berkeley

11:20–11:30 am EDT

Break

11:30 am–12:30 pm EDT

Mechanisms of attitude change
Moderator: Jocelyn Finlay, Harvard University

This session will focus on questions such as:

- What are the mechanisms by which changes in attitudes toward and opportunities for girls and women affect changes in attitudes toward and use of contraceptives (and vice versa)?
- What are the noneconomic benefits of changing social norms?
- What have we learned from recent experimental research?

Sajeda Amin, Population Council
Sarah Baird, George Washington University
Rajiv Rimal, Johns Hopkins University

12:30–1:00 pm EDT
Break

1:00–2:10 pm EDT
Foundation and agency programs and priorities
Moderator: Sunita Kishor, ICF

Althea Anderson, Hewlett Foundation
Benoit Kalasa, United Nations Population Fund
Tamara Kreinin, Packard Foundation
Afeefa Abdur-Rahman, Office of Population and Reproductive Health, USAID (Contractor)
Ann Starrs, Bill & Melinda Gates Foundation

2:10–3:30 pm EDT
Summary of key themes and next steps to move the field forward

Amy Tsui, Johns Hopkins University (emerita)
Sunita Kishor, ICF
Jocelyn Finlay, Harvard University
Alex Ezeh, Drexel University
Mayra Buvinic, United Nations Foundation
Nancy Birdsall, Center for Global Development
Ann Blanc, Steering Committee Chair, Population Council

3:30 pm EDT
Adjourn